Choosing a Bible

CHOOSING a BIBLE

For Worship, Teaching, Study,
Preaching, and Prayer

DONALD KRAUS

SEABURY BOOKS
An imprint of Church Publishing, Inc., New York

Library of Congress Cataloging-in-Publication Data

Kraus, Donald.
   Choosing a Bible : for worship, teaching, preaching, study, and prayer
/ Donald Kraus.
      p. cm.
   ISBN-13: 978-1-59627-043-5
   ISBN-10: 1-59627-043-8
   1. Bible. English–Versions. I. Title.

   BS455.K73 2006
   220.5'2–dc22

                                                            2006029163

Copyright information regarding the Bible translations quoted in this book may be found following the Quick Guide to Bible Translations.

Church Publishing, Inc.
445 Fifth Avenue
New York, NY 10016
www.churchpublishing.org

For Sue
"partner and co-worker"
(2 Corinthians 8.23)

❦ CONTENTS

Charts

⚜ ACKNOWLEDGMENTS

THE VAST MAJORITY of those who read the Bible are indebted above all to those laborers, mostly anonymous, who have undertaken the work of translating the complex literary collection known as "the Bible" into English. I am, most emphatically, among the readers whose knowledge of the Bible, if it required reading only in the original languages, would be severely truncated. First, therefore, let me thank all of those, named or not, who have carried out the work of translation that these pages discuss.

This is not a work of scholarship, but it nevertheless relies upon scholarly work. I therefore particularly acknowledge indebtedness to those scholars whose writings have helped me understand translation better: John R. Kohlenberger III, whose editorial skills in describing Bible translations are always enlightening; D. A. Carson, whose book *The Inclusive Language Debate* is a model for writing fairly about a controversial topic; and Mark L. Strauss, whose essay "Understanding New Testament Translation" in the *Evangelical Parallel New Testament* provides an intellectual underpinning for the following discussion. I also owe much to Albert Pietersma, who lucidly explains highly technical translation matters in his introduction to *A New English Translation of the Septuagint*, "To the Reader of NETS." The world of biblical scholarship eagerly awaits the full English Septuagint that Professor Pietersma and his colleagues have been laboring over for a decade or more.

Scott Meyer, of the Merritt Bookstore in Millbrook, New York, suggested that I explain the different sorts of Bible translations and what they were for. Mr. Meyer and the audience he assembled first heard the presentation that was the basis of this book. B. J. Smith, my colleague at Oxford University Press, later requested that I speak to her and to Oxford's sales and customer service team, and that gave me the chance to work through the presentation once again. The questions and comments I received from my hearers were invaluable in helping to shape this material.

Margaret Brown, my perceptive and enthusiastic friend, read drafts of these chapters and encouraged me during the process of rewriting and expanding my explanations. Cynthia Shattuck, of Church Publishing, Inc., has been the ideal editor. It is a particularly hazardous thing to edit another editor; Cynthia believed in this book even before I did, and her careful and considerate comments along the way have only served to make what I have written stronger and clearer. This book would not have come into existence without her constant help. Vicki Black carefully copyedited the text and attended to numerous details. I deeply thank them all.

Finally, as the dedication should show, I owe the most to my wife, Susan Kraus, whose continual support has marked our entire life together. Sue's careful reading of, and comments on, each stage of these explanations were invaluable in clarifying my thought and expression. More than this, however, was her unfailing belief that this was a project worth doing and one that could be of wide helpfulness to teachers and learners alike. I share that belief, and hope that readers will find it to be so.

AUGUST 2006

❧ PREFACE

AN ACQUAINTANCE ONCE told me about a time in his life when he looked into the possibility of becoming a professional chef. He was already a pretty good amateur cook — he still is — and he applied to a well-known cooking school. He filled out applications and scheduled an interview.

So far, everything was normal; it was the same as applying to college. But for the interview, the school asked him to bring his knives with him. Apparently, one chef can tell a good deal about another chef by examining his or her knives: their quality, their condition (both the extent to which they have been used, and how they have been cared for), and their variety.

I found this fascinating, but it also got me thinking. Many of us, in one way or another, are involved in presenting the Bible, in translation, to those who know little or nothing about it. What are the "knives" — the individual translations — that we could show someone to demonstrate how we go about studying or preaching or teaching? With what set of tools do we go to our tasks? How do we use them? Which ones could we tell others that they should own themselves, and which ones are optional? And most important of all, how do we understand — and explain — the differences in these basic teaching tools? Why are there so many translations of the Bible, and which ones are the right ones to use?

I wrote this book to help provide answers for such questions. For over twenty years, I have been professionally involved with Bible translations: assessing them, publishing them, describing them, defending them. I've had to think hard and continuously about them: why there are so many, why they vary so much from one another, and what we can and cannot do with them.

Return for a moment to my friend with his knives. No one who cooks, or who has even done kitchen duty while someone else cooked, would wonder, "Why are there so many different kinds of knives?" Mere experience makes clear that knives differ because of the uses to which they are put, and they are made specifically to meet one use or another. To be sure, in a pinch you can use some knives for tasks they were not designed to do — you *can* cut up a chicken with a paring knife — but it is not as easy as using the right tool. And there are "general purpose" knives that can be used in several different ways. But no one who is a serious cook will rely for long on a single knife, and for some tasks — slicing freshly baked bread, for instance — you need something designed for that purpose.

As we shall see, the same is true of Bible translations. There are "general purpose" translations that are suitable for study and for reading, and there are "specialized" translations — ones with specific goals and purposes in mind. The point is to learn enough about them to be able to apply the right translation to the right task. As with knives and cooking, the best way to do this is to use them and learn by experience. There is no substitute for wide reading in different translations. Gaining a sense of how they "wear," how they hold up under sustained attention, is invaluable. But it is also important to experience the different kinds of reading that different translations encourage or discourage.

Some translations, like the New American Standard Bible, are best for concentrated word-study; others, like the New Living Translation, are excellent for reading a narrative quickly. The New International Version or the New Revised Standard Version work well when read aloud, while the Contemporary English Version or The Message are very helpful for youth groups or people whose English-language skills are limited. Some, like The Message or the J. B. Phillips New Testament, make scenes and stories vivid, almost contemporary; others, like the Everett Fox or Robert Alter translations of the Hebrew Bible, give the reader a sense of participating in an ancient culture.

There is almost always something to be said in favor of any translation, and it is much more productive to understand the positive uses to which a particular version can be put than it is to expend energy in trying to tear a translation down. Almost every translation serves a purpose, and the best way to approach any one of them is to try to find out what that purpose is, and then determine whether the translation meets its intended goals or not. There are plenty of people who will tell you which translations are the "bad" ones — meaning the translations they themselves disapprove of. But wouldn't it be better to try to see how each translation is a "good" one, in its own way?

That is the goal of this book.

Chapter 1

✥ WHAT IS TRANSLATION?

WE ALL THINK we know what translation is. Translation is the act of rendering the words, thoughts, images, and ideas expressed in one language into another. Although it may be difficult in practice — hard words, idioms, unclear writing, and other such stumbling blocks may impede progress — and although it requires knowledge of at least two languages, we think the theory must be pretty straightforward. With grammars and dictionaries, we think, it must be possible to translate texts from one language to another and manage to get most of the meaning across. There must be a "best" way to translate any text, and if we can't read the original languages, we just have to find the "best" translation and use that. We may lose some "poetry," but we'll get more than the gist — we'll get what the original author intended us to get.

Such an attitude is harder to maintain once we have learned a foreign language — almost any foreign language. In the process of learning we come to recognize that there are nuances that escape us when we try to render one language into another. Sometimes it is necessary *not* to translate by the dictionary, but to consider a larger context and represent the author's *meaning,* not necessarily what the author literally *said.* In Romans 9.29, for example, Paul quotes Isaiah 1.9, a passage which in the original refers to "survivors" who are spared the destruction of Jerusalem (*sadir kim'at,* "a few escapees"). Paul, however, uses the Greek word that means "descendants" (*sperma,* "seed") instead of "survivors," thereby inadvertently

1

changing the sense of the passage. The point is not that, though we are destroyed, our progeny will live on; rather, it is that, though most of us are destroyed, enough will survive to form the basis of a new community. Most translations mistake the meaning here and translate "seed" or "descendants"; the New Revised Standard Version, however, correctly renders this "survivors," thereby clarifying Paul's argument that God has called a small group from the existing Jewish and Gentile communities (9.23–24).

The idea that there is only one right way to translate a text must evaporate when we realize how many translations of the Bible there really are. When we encounter this multiplicity of versions, either we can despair and withdraw into one favorite translation to the exclusion of all others, or we can wander at a loss, picking and choosing from among the great variety of Bibles available but never understanding what each one is trying to accomplish.

In working through a variety of Bible translations, however, we may also come to a better understanding of what translation truly is. In the following pages we will first be looking at a number of issues involved in translation, some general and some specific to translating the Bible. Following that overview, we will be looking at specific examples and illustrations of different translation strategies. We will be examining the reasons for the different approaches, and trying out the uses to which such different renditions can be put. And at the end, although we may still keep to our favorite translation for habitual reading, preaching, and teaching, we may have learned to expand our repertoires with a much wider choice of reading, and we will also be able to recommend different translations to different readers for different uses, depending on their abilities, desires, aims, ages, and education. For example, someone who has taken college or graduate school courses in literature may be perfectly comfortable with the translators' notes in the NET (New English Translation) Bible, which give many alternative nuances for translation choice. But a fourteen-year-old, or someone learning English as a second language, might much prefer the

Contemporary English Version, with its simpler vocabulary and minimal apparatus.

This prospect gives us the key to understanding what a translation is. Far from being the static, fixed result of a mechanical process, translation is a dynamic mediation, as much art as science, between the original language text and the language actually used by the audience. Furthermore, with a text like the Bible, originating in a distant time and place, "translation" necessarily involves more than verbal issues: matters of culture, belief, daily life, and so on also have to be taken into account.

LANGUAGES AND AUDIENCES

Any translation works with two languages: the original or "source" language, and the translated or "target" language. Similarly, it also works with two communities: the original audience for the text and the present-day audience. As we move into specific examples we will see how these four factors influence the results of the translation, but in a preliminary way we can say the following:

✝ A translation that treats the *source* language as primary takes an approach that is "word-for-word" or "literal." Such a translation of the Bible will try as far as possible to reproduce Greek or Hebrew language patterns in English. (We look at specific examples of this in chapter 6.)

✝ A translation that treats the *target* language as primary takes an approach that is "meaning-for-meaning" or "readable." Such a translation of the Bible tries to a greater or lesser extent to re-express in English what the original writer meant — not necessarily what the original writer literally said — in Greek or Hebrew. (Once again, we will look at specific examples in chapter 6.)

We might more easily grasp the difference between these two approaches if we think of a non-native but fluent speaker of English who still conceptualizes in another language and then turns the ideas into English, versus a native English-speaker, fluent in a foreign language, who listens to an explanation in that language and then restates it in standard, idiomatic English. In the one case we have a foreigner speaking English, with perhaps some echoes of the foreign language; in the other, an English-speaker whose ideas came from elsewhere but whose language is her own.

As far as the audiences are concerned — the original, ancient audience for a biblical text and the present-day readers for whom the translation is intended — their influence on the translation process is more subtle, but in some ways more momentous.

⸎ When a translation treats the source language as primary, it often simply accepts those aspects of the text having to do with the original audience and setting. For a contemporary audience, the result will be an experience of the text that is *exotic,* emphasizing its origins in an ancient culture very different from our own. It is important to recognize that such an experience of the text as exotic and ancient *is not the way the original audience experienced it.*

⸎ When a translation treats the target language as primary, it may also look at the possible ways the original audience could have experienced the text and come up with approaches that will provide an analogous experience for a contemporary audience. Here we must recognize that such an approach to the text may *slide past the need to acknowledge cultural differences* between the original and contemporary audiences, and may also create a translation that rapidly *loses its relevance* as its contemporary references themselves become outdated.

AREAS OF MEANING

In undertaking any translation, it is necessary to deal both with the variety of meanings — the "semantic range" — of any given word we are trying to translate from the source language, and also with the full set of meanings of the word we are using in the target language. These ranges of meaning between words in one language and words in another generally do not overlap exactly. This can be made a little clearer if we consider the relationship between words within one language. To do so, we will look at three different ways of expressing meaning: synonyms, glosses, and definitions.

A *synonym* is a word that is deemed to be equivalent in meaning to another word. As its name suggests, a "synonym" is "another name for the same thing." But a little thought and experimentation will show that in fact exact synonyms — two words with exactly the same meanings — are rare, perhaps nonexistent. For instance, in reading a medical book we might come across the word "febrile." If we were to ask a physician for the meaning of "febrile," we would probably be told, "It means 'feverish.'" Thus, "febrile" and "feverish" are synonyms. But they are not exact synonyms, because we cannot use "febrile" wherever we use "feverish." We can't say of a colleague, "He's working at a febrile pace." The range of meaning of "feverish" is larger than the range of meaning of "febrile."

A *gloss* is a short definition in context. We could gloss "crawling" as "moving on hands and knees." But in context — as in the sentence, "The sidewalk was crawling with ants" — we would have to gloss it as "covered," and moreover we would probably have to add the information that what the sidewalk is covered with is itself moving. "Moving on hands and knees" is a good gloss for "crawling" only in certain contexts: "The sidewalk was moving on hands and knees with ants" does not make sense.

The definition of a word is ideally its complete range of meaning. To get an idea of the complexity involved in this, we can consider the longest definition in the original edition of the *Oxford English Dictionary:* the one for the word "set." The OED was originally called *A New English Dictionary on Historical Principles,* and its guiding philosophy was to define each word completely according to actual contextual usage, in all its meanings. This meant first collecting and then arranging significant citations for a given word, and distinguishing between their shades of meaning.

"Set" is both a noun and a verb. For the noun the dictionary ended up with two main divisions, one being words that indicate placement or arrangement. These ranged from a largely archaic sense preserved in the noun "sunset" (the quality or condition of descending) to such matters as the arrangement of plantings. The second main division of the noun covered various meanings of groups in general, whether persons or things: a "social set" or a "set of china," for instance. These two substantive areas of meaning covered 47 different subsidiary meanings.

The range of meanings for "set" as a verb is even more complex. The dictionary arranged the senses under twelve general headings ("to descend," "to place," and various meanings in combination with prepositions — "set off," "set out," "set up," and so forth), leading to 147 subsidiary senses, one of which itself — "set up" — could be distinguished into 44 separate uses. The entire definition, both noun and verb, covered 68 columns.

Clearly, in any translation from English to another language, there could be no single equivalent for such a word. Even if the translator held to a very strict word-for-word approach, it would be necessary to translate such a word as "set" contextually, and therefore to admit in principle that "meaning-for-meaning" translation is a legitimate approach.

These examples should make clear that words can have a great range of meaning, and, therefore, that any translation needs to take into account not just a "core" meaning but a full range. And once we realize this, we will also realize that when translating from one language to another, it is likely to be the case that this wider range of meaning will be one of the things we will be trying to translate — and that it is unlikely that words in different languages will have exactly overlapping ranges of meaning. We will have to choose, in fact, between translating *what was said* (that is, the literal words that were spoken or written, translated into the target language) and *what was meant* (the intent behind the words, re-thought and re-expressed).

A very elementary example of this occurs in John 3.8. In this verse a key term appears three times (once as a verb, twice as a noun): the word *pneuma* (noun) or *pneo* (verb). Here, in the

New American Standard Bible translation, is the verse with the key words highlighted:

> The **wind blows** where it wishes and you hear the sound of it, but do not know where it comes from and where it is going; so is every one who is born of the **Spirit**.

"Wind" and "Spirit" are the same word in Greek, but it is impossible to translate this verse into English without using different words for the occurrences of the same Greek word.

A recent example of the value of meaning-for-meaning translation took place in late 1956. In a meeting with Americans in Moscow, the leader of the Soviet Union, Nikita S. Khrushchev, made a remark that was reported around the world. Referring to the struggle for political supremacy between the United States and the USSR, he said, "We will bury you." Khrushchev was speaking in Russian, and his words were rendered into English by a translator on the spot. They caused an immediate outcry in America, because many who heard or read them took them as a threat: "We will destroy you." The hearers, in other words, took "bury" to be a synonym for "kill."

But it appears that Khrushchev was not making that kind of a threat. In Russian usage, a strong subsidiary meaning for "bury" was "outlive." A similar meaning occurs in English when we refer to someone who has "buried" a spouse — it is not an accusation of murder. In English, this sense is fairly uncommon and somewhat old-fashioned. Therefore, and also presumably because of the level of hostility between the United States and the USSR, most Americans leapt to the conclusion that Khrushchev was making a lethal threat, whereas he was probably intending to say simply, "We will outlast you." The translator in this case rendered *what he said* rather than *what he meant*. Clearly, the approach a translator takes *matters*.

AVAILABLE BIBLE TRANSLATIONS

Before we look more closely at various approaches to translation, we need to be somewhat familiar with the broad range of Bible translations available to readers today. The following chart lists, in alphabetical order, translations that are generally available, and gives their basic orientation (usually toward a particular religious or denominational perspective), whether they were translated by a committee or an individual, the extent of their canonical contents, and whether they are American or British in style or exist in editions reflecting both American and British usage.

The issue of whether a translation is the result of an individual effort or a committee tends to influence how adventurous it is. Committees build in review and revision procedures for their translation efforts. This helps to guard against too much idiosyncratic translation, but it also tends to flatten the resulting text and neutralize efforts to attain an interesting style. Committees avoid oddity and errors — you are not lost in the depths of Death Valley — but they also avoid daring, if defensible, phrasing — neither do you ascend the heights of Everest. Everything is Kansas when created by committee. (The one major exception is the King James Version.) Translations by individuals, on the other hand, can soar into poetry, or at least into literary prose, but they can also take distinctly minority approaches. For example, J. B. Phillips, as shown below (p. 66) in the translation of the beginning of the Gospel of John, tried to convey what was meant by the Greek word *logos,* rather than simply translating it "word." As many readers have agreed since, his choice was interesting but not persuasive. Whenever you are using a translation by an individual, you should always check it against an established committee-created version before relying on it in an argument or sermon.

GENERALLY AVAILABLE BIBLE TRANSLATIONS

Translation	Religious Orientation	Translated by	Contents	Style
Five Books of Moses (Alter)	Jewish	Individual	Hebrew Bible (OT)	American
Contemporary English Version*	Ecumenical	Committee	Apocrypha / Deuterocanon	American
Douay-Rheims	Catholic	Committee	Deuterocanon	British
English Standard Version	Evangelical / Protestant	Committee	No Apocrypha	American
Five Books of Moses (Fox)	Jewish	Individual	Hebrew Bible (OT)	American
Holman Christian Standard Bible	Evangelical / Protestant	Committee	No Apocrypha	American
Jerusalem Bible / New Jerusalem Bible	Catholic	Committee	Deuterocanon	British
King James Version	Protestant	Committee	Apocrypha	British
The Holy Bible (Knox)	Catholic	Individual	Deuterocanon	British
The Message	Evangelical / Protestant	Individual	No Apocrypha	American
The Bible (Moffatt)	Protestant	Individual	No Apocrypha	British
New American Bible*	Catholic	Committee	Deuterocanon	American
New American Standard Bible	Evangelical / Protestant	Committee	No Apocrypha	American
New Century Version	Evangelical / Protestant	Committee	No Apocrypha	American
New English Bible / Revised English Bible*	Ecumenical	Committee	Apocrypha / Deuterocanon	British
New English Translation Bible	Evangelical / Protestant	Committee	No Apocrypha	American
New International Version	Evangelical / Protestant	Committee	No Apocrypha	American
New Jewish Publication Society Tanakh	Jewish	Committee	Hebrew Bible (OT)	American
New King James Version	Evangelical / Protestant	Committee	No Apocrypha	American
New Living Translation*	Evangelical / Protestant	Committee	Apocrypha / Deuterocanon	American
New Revised Standard Version* / RSV	Ecumenical	Committee	Apocrypha / Deuterocanon	Amer / British
New Testament in Modern English (Phillips)	Protestant	Individual	NT only	British
Today's English Version	Ecumenical	Committee	Apocrypha / Deuterocanon	American
Today's New International Version*	Evangelical / Protestant	Committee	No Apocrypha	American

*Inclusive language with regard to human beings

DIFFERING CANONS

The issue of the varying canonical contents of various Bible translations is addressed in the following chart, giving various approaches to the canon of the Hebrew Bible. (The contents and order of the New Testament are not in dispute among various Christian bodies.) The Hebrew Bible/ Old Testament varies depending on which group is using it. The Jewish Bible has a different order than Christian Bibles do; even when the contents are the same, the Protestant Christian Old Testament is the Hebrew Bible in the arrangement found in the Septuagint, the ancient Greek translation of the Hebrew Bible.

As we have seen, the choice of a translation will partly be influenced by one's need for a particular canon — Protestant, Catholic, or Orthodox Christian, or Jewish. The Jewish canon, as noted, is identical in contents, though not in order, to the Protestant Old Testament. This difference in order is important because all versions of the Christian Old Testament end with the prophetic book of Malachi, seen as foreshadowing John the Baptist with its dire ending:

> Lo, I will send you the prophet Elijah before the great and terrible day of the LORD comes. He will turn the hearts of parents to their children and the hearts of children to their parents, so that I will not come and strike the land with a curse. (4.5-6, NRSV)

In contrast, the Jewish Bible ends with 2 Chronicles, narrating the return of the people to their land after the Babylonian exile. The final words of the Hebrew Bible are the decree of Cyrus of Persia:

> "The LORD, the God of heaven, has given me all the kingdoms of the earth, and he has charged me to build him a house at Jerusalem, which is in Judah. Whoever is among you of all his people, may the LORD his God be with him! Let him go up." (36.23, NRSV)

The Catholic Old Testament includes additional books (Tobit, Judith, 1 and 2 Maccabees, the Wisdom of Solomon, the Wisdom of Jesus ben Sirach [Ecclesiasticus], Baruch) and longer versions of two other books: Esther, which includes six additional passages not present in the Hebrew version, and Daniel, which includes three additions: the Prayer of Azariah and the Song of the Three Youths, in chapter 3, and, at the end of the book, two stories: that of Susanna and of Daniel, Bel, and the Snake. Orthodox Christian canons include all of the additional books that Catholics include, plus some or all of the following: 1 and 2 Esdras, the Prayer of Manasseh, Psalm 151, 3 Maccabees, and (in an appendix), 4 Maccabees. All of these additional books are contained in the ancient Greek version of the Hebrew Bible, the Septuagint, which had contents larger than what became the Hebrew Bible. Because the early Christian church used the Greek Bible, these books were included from an early period, and were only discarded from the canon by Protestant Reformers in the sixteenth century. Anglicans and Lutherans use some of the Apocryphal books — the Catholic canon, plus 1 and 2 Esdras and the Prayer of Manasseh — in their lectionaries and canticles.

Thus, in addition to translation approaches, reading level, and style, we need to take account of denominational and religious characteristics of translations — both in the contents of the individual books of the Bible, and in their order — when choosing a translation for a particular audience.

DIFFERING CANONS OF THE
HEBREW BIBLE / OLD TESTAMENT

Jewish Canon	Protestant Canon	Roman Catholic / Orthodox Canon
Torah (TEACHING)	PENTATEUCH (Five Books of Moses)	PENTATEUCH
Genesis	Genesis	Genesis
Exodus	Exodus	Exodus
Leviticus	Leviticus	Leviticus
Numbers	Numbers	Numbers
Deuteronomy	Deuteronomy	Deuteronomy
Nevi'im (PROPHETS)	HISTORIES	HISTORIES
Former Prophets		
Joshua	Joshua	Joshua
Judges	Judges	Judges
	Ruth	Ruth
Samuel (1 & 2)	1 & 2 Samuel	1 & 2 Samuel
Kings (1 & 2)	1 & 2 Kings	1 & 2 Kings
	1 & 2 Chronicles	1 & 2 Chronicles
	Ezra	Ezra
	Nehemiah	Nehemiah
		Tobit
		Judith
	Esther	Esther (longer version)
		1 & 2 Maccabees
Latter Prophets	POETICAL AND	POETICAL &
Isaiah	WISDOM BOOKS	WISDOM BOOKS
Jeremiah	Job	Job
Ezekiel	Psalms	Psalms
The Twelve	Proverbs	Proverbs
Hosea	Ecclesiastes	Ecclesiastes
Joel	Song of Songs	Song of Songs
Amos		Wisdom of Solomon
Obadiah		Sirach
Jonah		(Ecclesiasticus)
Micah		
Nahum		
Habakkuk		
Zephaniah		
Haggai		
Zechariah		
Malachi		

DIFFERING CANONS
continued

Jewish Canon	Protestant Canon	Roman Catholic / Orthodox Canon
Ketubim (WRITINGS)	PROPHETS	PROPHETS
Psalms	Isaiah	Isaiah
Proverbs	Jeremiah	Jeremiah
Job	Lamentations	Lamentations
Five Scrolls		Baruch (with Letter
Song of Songs		of Jeremiah)
Ruth	Ezekiel	Ezekiel
Lamentations	Daniel	Daniel (longer version)
Ecclesiastes	Hosea	Hosea
Esther	Joel	Joel
Daniel	Amos	Amos
Ezra-Nehemiah	Obadiah	Obadiah
Chronicles (1 & 2)	Jonah	Jonah
	Micah	Micah
	Nahum	Nahum
	Habakkuk	Habakkuk
	Zephaniah	Zephaniah
	Haggai	Haggai
	Zechariah	Zechariah
	Malachi	Malachi
The Jewish canon does not include any books of the Apocrypha	THE APOCRYPHA	ORTHODOX DEUTEROCANON
	1 & 2 Esdras	1 & 2 Esdras
	Tobit	Prayer of Manasseh
	Judith	Psalm 151
	Esther (with additions)	3 Maccabees
	Wisdom of Solomon	4 Maccabees (in an
	Ecclesiasticus (Sirach)	appendix)
	Baruch	
	Letter of Jeremiah (Baruch chp. 6)	
	Prayer of Azariah and Song of Three	
	Daniel and Susanna	
	Daniel, Bel, and Snake	
	Prayer of Manasseh	
	1 & 2 Maccabees	

Chapter 2

SOURCE AND TARGET LANGUAGES

THE DOZENS OF translations of the Bible that publishers now offer can seem to be simply an indistinguishable mass of versions that have little or no relationship with each other. In fact, however, it is possible to view them together, so to speak, and see where they stand as compared with one another. To do this, we can arrange them on a spectrum according to the relationship they have to the two languages involved: the source, or original, language of the document, and the target, or translation, language.

The following chart shows how some of the main current translations fall (in general) on a spectrum that ranges from the most literal approach to translation, on the left, to the most dynamic or functional, on the right. Note that the translations tend to cluster in the middle of the spectrum. This is not coincidental: most translations are specifically intended to be as readable as they possibly can be while still remaining fairly wedded to a formal or literal approach to word choices. This means that these translations are good, usable versions that can be widely read in churches or privately, but can also be used in the classroom or in contexts where the users must pay attention to specific words or phrases, such as in commentaries.

Note also the contrasting pairs of characteristics at either end of the spectrum. One difference in translation approach influences vocabulary choices. At the formal end is consistency, or lexical concordance: the effort on the part of the translators to use the same word in English for the same underlying Greek or Hebrew word. At the functional end is contextual meaning: the approach that looks at the specific way in which the word is used in context in each passage, and then tries to come up with an English equivalent that represents a similar semantic range. This difference in translation approaches is shown in various translations from the letter to the Ephesians 1.3 below in chapter 6 (pp. 69–70).

Another difference in translation approach involves sentence structure. At the formal end is syntactical correspondence: the reproduction, as far as is possible, of the original language's sentence structure and length in the translation. At the functional end is idiomatic rendering: the use of common English-language syntax to recreate the meaning of the original language sentence in a new structure. The difference this can make in various translations is shown below in a comparison of different approaches to translating the beginning of the letter to the Romans (pp. 67–69).

BIBLE TRANSLATION SPECTRUM

Source Language						Target Language
Formal equivalent						*Dynamic equivalent*
Word-for-word						*Meaning-for-meaning*
Literal or direct translation						*Functional translation*
Tends toward interlinear translation						*Tends toward paraphrase*
Consistency (lexical concordance)						*Contextual meaning*
Syntactical correspondence						*Idiomatic rendering*
NASB	NKJV	RSV	NRSV	TEV	NLT	The Message
NET Bible	KJV	ESV	NIV	CEV	Moffatt	Phillips
Fox	Douay	HCSB	NAB	NEB	NCV	
Alter			NJPS	REB	JB/NJB	
			TNIV		Knox	

FORMAL EQUIVALENCE

At one end of this spectrum are word-for-word or formal equivalent versions, translations where the form and characteristics of the source language play a controlling role. The "pure" form of such a translation is an interlinear rendering, where each word in the source language is represented by a corresponding word, in the exact same word order, in the target language. The common French phrase abbreviated R.S.V.P. — *Répondez, s'il vous plait* — meaning "Please answer" would be rendered "Respond, if it you pleases" in an interlinear version. (For an interlinear rendering of the Lord's Prayer, see chapter 6, p. 58.) Interlinear renderings are not translations, since the result is not really comprehensible on its own in the target language, but there are two aspects of the interlinear approach that characterize formal translations.

One is syntactical correspondence. In translations that take this approach, the translators make every effort possible to reproduce the sentence structure of the original language. The result of this kind of translation approach is that some passages in the translation will have very complex sentence structures, often ones not characteristic of the target language. Four renderings of Romans 1.1-7 below (pp. 67-69) contrast the formal approach — which reproduces the single Greek sentence as a single English sentence — with the idiomatic approach, which renders it as several English sentences. The effort to reproduce Greek syntax generally means that the reading level of formal translations is high.

Another characteristic of formal translations is their effort to achieve lexical consistency. This means that, whenever possible, such translations use the same English word to represent an underlying Greek or Hebrew word, regardless of the context, the form of the word, or its shades of meaning. (See chapter 6, pp. 69-70, for an example from Ephesians 1.3, where the repetition of Greek words for "bless" is reproduced in some translations, but not in others.)

FUNCTIONAL EQUIVALENCE

At the other end of the spectrum are meaning-for-meaning translations; these are also called dynamic equivalent or functional equivalent versions, translations in which the target language takes the dominant role. These translations strive, as far as possible while attending to the original Hebrew or Greek texts, to recreate the meaning and effect of the originals, rather than to reproduce their structure and terminology strictly. The extreme form of this translation approach is the paraphrase, which can shade into a "retelling" — in other words, not a translation at all, not a rendering that makes any reference to the original languages, but a new rendering of narrative or parable into a contemporary idiom. *The Cotton Patch Gospels,* for example, contain renderings of the parables of Jesus in the vernacular of the American South.

Unlike a paraphrase, a functional equivalent translation *is* still a translation. In contrast to the formal translation approach, however, the emphasis has shifted: the translators attempt to find contemporary language that will convey the same sense to readers today as the original text did to its first audiences. Functional equivalent translations make no effort to represent the syntax of the original where that would result in sentence structure that is not idiomatic in the target language. (See the example from Romans 1.1-7, pp. 67-69.) Nor do they strive for lexical consistency, if the range of meaning of an underlying term needs to be represented by different English terms. (See the example from Ephesians 1.3, pp. 69-70.) They are therefore, as these extracts show, characterized by idiomatic rendering (as opposed to syntactical correspondence) and by contextual meaning (instead of lexical consistency). Idiomatic rendering is the effort to create a natural-sounding sentence structure in English. Contextual meaning is the effort to represent as closely as possible the meaning of a term in its context, rather than using a single English equivalent for each occurrence of a Greek or Hebrew word.

ADVANTAGES AND DISADVANTAGES
OF EACH APPROACH

Although people have argued for the superiority of one approach to translation over the other, the fact is that both approaches have advantages and disadvantages.

Functional equivalent translations are readable and idiomatic. This is a great advantage particularly for those who are new to reading the Bible. Narratives in functional equivalent translations — the gospels, the history books, Esther, the book of Acts — can be read *as narratives,* making them inviting for the novice and giving even experienced readers the sense of a story moving forward strongly on the power of its narrative flow. In addition, since functional equivalent translations tend to use idiomatic expressions in the target language, the reader is not aware of being kept at a distance from the text.

In contrast, formal equivalent translations are precise. This makes them excellent for exact study, for explanations of doctrines based on biblical texts, and for commentary. Their efforts to use the same or similar English words for the same underlying Hebrew or Greek words in the original text makes it easy for those engaged in word-studies — teachers or commentators familiar with the Hebrew or Greek texts — to point to other passages that can enlighten readers who do not know the original languages. It is also the case that formal translations accurately represent the biblical text as the product of an ancient and foreign culture, one that is distant from our own.

This last point is worth emphasizing. It is often the case, when a new formal translation appears, that reviewers in newspapers and magazines will call attention to the fact that the translation presents the Bible as an ancient text. For example, in a review of Robert Alter's translation of *The Five Books of Moses* that also takes into account Everett Fox's translation published under the same title, the reviewer Judith Shulevitz calls attention to the fact that both versions, in their approach to the Hebrew text, "preserve its key words and archaic texture."[1] And this is certainly true. The Bible *is* an ancient text, and such translations make that clear. But what such reviewers miss is the following: For the original audience of the biblical text, the text was precisely *not* an ancient text. It was utterly contemporary. Therefore, by making clear that the Bible is from a very different time and place, such translations are both truer to the text and falser to the audience's experience of it.

Ms. Shulevitz also attributes to Professor Alter more of an innovative approach to translation than his method deserves. His is essentially a highly formal, word-for-word approach. In the review, Ms. Shulevitz calls attention to Professor Alter's literal rendering of the Hebrew idiom meaning "pay attention to": the phrase "listen [or 'hearken'] to the voice" of someone. She claims that by translating this literally (and always in the same words) when it occurs in the Genesis narratives, Professor Alter has made available to English-language readers linguistic echoes in the Hebrew text that they would have been unaware of before. It is true that most modern translations render the meaning rather than the exact phrasing of the Hebrew, but this is not due to sloppiness but to a different approach to translation. In fact, the British Revised Version of 1885, following the King James Version, also preserved this idiom, and the same echoes of the phrase "listen to one's voice" ("hearken unto her voice," Gen. 21.12; "obey my voice," Gen. 27.43) that are present in Professor Alter's version are present in the nineteenth-century English one. (Ms. Shulevitz notes this with regard to the King James Version, but she criticizes it for allowing any variation at all, maintaining that the translation should retain "listen" at all times. This is an approach that would severely limit any translator in taking account of contextual meaning.) This does not mean that the Revised Version influenced Professor Alter; rather, it means that both he and the committee that produced the Revised Version chose to undertake the same kind of translation: a highly formal one.

A functional equivalent rendering of the text that pays attention to English idiom is *in some ways* a more accurate rendition of the way the original audience experienced the text than is one that is scrupulously accurate in translating every last word with its original linguistic or cultural references still clinging to it. At the very least, such a version gives modern-day readers the experience of the text that the original readers or hearers would have had: that of someone speaking to them, or writing to them, in everyday terms. But "everyday terms" does not mean any effort to blunt what the text is saying; it only means that alien cultural references should not get in the way of what the text is truly demanding. If the original audience would have viewed something as strange, shocking, or unnatural, an audience today should also see it in the same way.

Any translation, therefore, has to present the *content* of the text as clearly as possible. Biblical narratives with shocking or distressing elements, or strong moral denunciations of human behavior, must not be obscured, no matter what translation approach is used. The issue is one of the form of words in which such matters are presented. The story of the near-sacrifice of Isaac (Genesis 22) or the murder and dismemberment of the concubine (Judges 19) should inspire dismay and horror in any version. And, in general, they do so.

1. *New York Times Book Review* (October 17, 2004): 8–9.

Chapter 3

❦ ORIGINAL AND CONTEMPORARY AUDIENCES

IN TRANSLATING FROM one language to another where we can assume that both works arise from the same general cultural background, translators do not usually have to pay much attention to the specific character of the original audience for the work being translated. A modern French novel that alludes to World War II or to Brigitte Bardot can be rendered in English without laborious paraphrase or explanatory footnotes referring to the Battle of the Bulge or French cinema of the 1950s and 60s. The translators can generally assume that the English-speaking audience, even if some or all of its members have never been to France, shares enough background with the French audience to make explanations redundant.

When there is less correspondence between the backgrounds of the audiences, there is more need for explanation. For instance, look at Leo Tolstoy's short story, "How Much Land Does a Man Need?" This narrative, almost an extended parable about a man ultimately destroyed by his greed for land, does not have much "local color," nor does it spend much time on description or characterization. In one place, however, Tolstoy includes an obscure reference. In the setting of the final episode, the "land of the Bashkirs," where the protagonist will meet his fate, he and his hosts drink *kumiss* (it is significant that this word is usually left untranslated). Therefore, most versions of the story need to explain to the non-Russian reader that *kumiss* is fermented mare's milk.

Clearly, when the original audience for a text and the audience for a translation come from widely separated cultures, times, and historical backgrounds — when they are separated not only by language but by history, culture, economic system, and many other factors — all of these aspects of the original audience's expectations and assumptions can affect what has to be done in translation. Such is the case with the Bible.

THE MATTER OF BIBLICAL STYLES

The Bible is a complex collection of writings. It was put together over the course of more than one thousand years: the earliest sections of the Hebrew Bible are generally agreed to go back to the time of David or even before, in the neighborhood of 1000 BCE, and perhaps one or two centuries before that. At the other end, the latest books of the New Testament were written probably between 90 and 125 CE. It was written and collected, therefore, over a span of time that is the equivalent of a work that was begun when Charlemagne was crowned Holy Roman Emperor (800 CE) and finished during the presidential election of 2000 CE. Furthermore, individual books within the Bible have histories of development that can be very complex. The book of the prophet Isaiah, for instance, was assembled over a period of two centuries or more — roughly equivalent to something that was begun at the American Revolution and completed in 2006.

As complex as the Bible's composition history is, that is not the only factor involved. For the various biblical books, audiences range from nomadic pastoralists to settled city dwellers, and from the most unfortunate and poverty-stricken to the very wealthy and the ruling classes. The types of writing that it contains are equally varied: short stories, historical narratives, chronicles and annals, legends and fables, various kinds of poetry, pithy sayings, and extended meditations. It addresses matters of the highest abstraction and of timeless interest, as well as those of the fleeting moment and the most local concern. The tone also varies: from earthy, even vulgar, to exalted and highly literary. And the abilities of the various writers also show considerable range: from highly trained rhetoricians to those barely literate in a language that is obviously not their native tongue.

Taking all of this into account in a translation, and trying to reproduce the effect (even if we could fully understand the effect) of the original, would produce a hodge-podge that would leave no one satisfied. Consider, for example, the phrase in the Revelation to John that is usually translated as "who is and who was and who is to come" (1.4). Rendered literally, this would be "the being, the was, and the coming" — in other words, it is both ungrammatical and unclear. The Revelation to John is difficult enough to read and understand; any efforts to render it literally, outside the context of a scholarly exegesis, would make it almost impossible for general readers.

All translations tend to even out the styles of the different biblical books. To produce a usable translation, in fact, it is necessary to do so. Hebrew poetry, which tends to be extremely compressed, must be "filled in" to make it comprehensible. Such a work as Job, with its obscure vocabulary and loan-words, would come out in English sounding, perhaps, like a modern poet imitating Shakespeare — or perhaps like James Joyce.

THE PROBLEM OF THE "ORIGINAL AUDIENCE"

There is another factor that comes into play for translations of the Bible. It is, at this point, almost impossible to arrive at a conception of what the "original audience" was for many of the biblical texts, and what that original audience might have known. In Proverbs, for example, was the original audience young male students? Scribes? Courtiers who collected sayings of the wise? Some combination of these? In Genesis, was the original audience aware of the ancient Near Eastern mythological background to the story of the Flood?

Besides these difficulties of determining who the original audience was and what it knew about the text or expected to hear, there are further complications. In many biblical passages, in the prophets for example, texts spoken or written for one audience were remembered and used again for later audiences in different situations. They were often adapted or revised to make them fit the new situation.

For example, in Amos 1.1 we are given regnal information that dates the book to the first half of the eighth century BCE. (The reigns of Josiah and Jeroboam effectively bracket the book as covering no more than the period from 788, when Jeroboam began to reign, until 733, when Uzziah died.) But Amos 9.11-15 refers to the period between 586 BCE, when Jerusalem was destroyed, and the late sixth century, when the Babylonian exile came to an end. Similarly, Isaiah 24.10-13, a passage which occurs in the part of the book dealing with events of the late eighth century, refers obliquely to the destruction of Babylon, which took place in 539 BCE — almost two hundred years later.

These are not simply matters of "predicting the future," as if the prophets were speaking under inspiration to inform an audience of what will happen centuries later. The texts give no clue that they are referring to a time different from that within their surrounding contexts. In such cases, there is apparently an overlap between audiences that are separated from each other by generations. Thus, the idea of an original audience is effectively irrecoverable.

THE PROBLEM OF THE "CONTEMPORARY AUDIENCE"

Finally, there is the question of the audience for which the translation is intended. Translators of the Bible are inevitably brought face-to-face with the fact that there is not simply *one* contemporary audience — there are many. Translations are undertaken for specific denominations, specific age groups, specific uses; for Catholics, Protestants, Jews; for teenagers or young adult seekers; for classroom study or reading aloud. How does this differentiation of audiences affect translation? In several ways.

First, it affects vocabulary choices. A translation intended for scholarly commentary or intensive study is likely to use a larger vocabulary than one intended for teenagers, children, or those for whom English is not their native language.

Second, it affects sentence structure. The syntax of a translation meant to be read aloud in religious services, or to oneself for devotional purposes, will be simpler than one meant for a commentary.

Third, it affects technical terminology. The Bible includes references to agricultural implements and practices, for instance ("winnowing forks," "threshing floors") and religious objects ("altar," "phylacteries") that are unfamiliar to many modern audiences. Denominational differences also come into play. The Greek term *episkopos* is often rendered "bishop," especially in translations produced by or intended for Catholics and Anglicans. "Bishop," however, is not really a translation of *episkopos;* it is the Greek word itself, transliterated into modern English by way of Latin and Old English, and furthermore pronounced corruptly. To translate *episkopos* one should render it "overseer" or "superintendent." In 1 Timothy 3.1–2, for instance, the King James Version uses "bishop," whereas contemporary translations from more evangelical origins (such as the New International Version and the New American Standard Bible) use "overseer." Other translations — such as the Contemporary English Version and The Message — use a more general term, such as "church official" or "leader." Still others, adopting a view that orders of ministry were not fixed in the early church, use "elder" (the New Century Version and the New Living Translation, for example) both here and in 5.17, where the Greek word is not *episkopos* but *presbyteros.* The New Century Version does not call attention to the underlying language difference; the New Living Translation does, but neither one openly makes clear that it is translating according to a specific understanding of polity.

The audience may also affect grammatical representation. To make a point in a scholarly monograph, a translator may render a biblical phrase or sentence in deliberately ungrammatical English. Likewise, in highly formal translations, which aim for syntactical correspondence, this will often be carried to the point of reproducing a flawed or incomplete sentence. In a literary or meaning-for-meaning translation, on the other hand, such stylistic roughness tends to be smoothed out. For instance, in Romans 5.12-13, it is quite clear that the beginning of the sentence is broken off and a new thought intrudes, leaving out the completion of the sentence. Here is the passage in the New American Standard Bible translation:

> Therefore, just as through one man sin entered into the world, and death through sin, and so death spread to all men, because all sinned — for until the Law sin was in the world, but sin is not imputed when there is no law.

The completion of the first part of this thought, along the lines of "so through one man came righteousness, and therefore life," or words to that effect, is clearly missing. Freer translations tend to treat this as an assertion standing on its own, as in the Contemporary English Version:

> Adam sinned, and that sin brought death into the world. Now everyone has sinned, and so everyone must die. Sin was in the world before the Law came. But no record of sin was kept, because there was no Law.

The translation has made the passage smoother, but at the expense of conveying what a more formal translation can get across: that of a man thinking on his feet, interrupting himself, and going off on a tangent — in fact, that of a real human being grappling with a whole new way of thinking about salvation. Here, paradoxically, the formal approach brings us closer to Paul than does the functional approach.

Chapter 4

❦ WHAT HAPPENS WHEN THE BIBLE QUOTES ITSELF?

THERE IS A traditional (and no doubt apocryphal) story of an old woman who was taken, for the first time in her life, to the theater to see a performance of *Hamlet*. When she was asked, after the play, what she thought of it, she remarked that the story was good enough, but the author should not have relied on so many famous quotations when writing his dialogue.

We are all used to the practice of quoting or alluding to well-known texts, or to lines or phrases from performances (not primarily plays, in our culture, but movies, television shows, comedians, popular songs, commercials, political speeches, and so on). Sometimes these references are only catch-phrases that flourish for a while and then die away; sometimes, as with literary allusions, they are more lasting. *The Sound and the Fury* is a quotation from *Macbeth*; *For Whom the Bell Tolls,* from a sermon of John Donne. We can all think of many instances, trivial and profound.

The Bible, too, is filled with "famous quotations," but they are largely echoes of itself. Sometimes these are allusions: Isaiah, in assuring the exiled Israelites of God's continuing care, refers to events of the Exodus narrative (Exodus 14 and 15):

Thus says the LORD,
  who makes a way in the sea,
  a path in the mighty waters,
who brings out chariot and horse,
  army and warrior;
they lie down, they cannot rise,
they are extinguished, quenched like a wick....
                                            (Is. 43.16–17, NRSV)

Sometimes they are direct quotations: in his letter to the Romans, Paul joins together two quotations from Hosea (parts of 2.23 and 1.10, altered):

As indeed he says in Hosea,
  "Those who were not my people I will call 'my people,'
    and her who was not beloved I will call 'beloved.'"
  "And in the very place where it was said to them,
    'You are not my people,'
    there they shall be called children of the living God."
                                            (Rom. 9.25–26, NRSV)

Matthew, in his gospel, includes ten quotations which he introduces by some form of the phrase, "This was to fulfill what was spoken by the Lord through the prophet... " (for instance, 1.22; 2.15). Often, however, these references to other biblical passages consist of previously used words or phrases in new contexts. As with any characteristic of a text, such verbal echoes are an aspect that must be considered when translating. But to consider this aspect does not necessarily mean to apply any rule or practice unimaginatively. In most cases these verbal echoes should be retained, so that the English reader can respond both to the original context and to the new one.

There are, however, situations in which problems can arise. One is the kind of situation in which a phrase in its new context, *as translated into English,* is only a fair representation of the meaning. The second is the situation that arises when the later text, in order to preserve its verbal echo, becomes a controlling factor in the translation of an earlier text, and results in a mistranslation or a less than adequate rendition. Here are two examples that require some care on the part of the translator.

"SON OF MAN"

In Daniel 7.13 the author describes an enigmatic figure in a vision with the phrase "one like a son of man" (*c'bar-enosh;* the phrase occurs in the Aramaic portion of the book). Within its original context, it may be that the writer was trying to convey something like "resembling a man." Later in Daniel (10.16, 18), similar language is used about angels. It is possible that an angel is meant here as well, and if so, the intent of the phrase would be "a non-human being in human form." The language is hesitant, as if to show the seer's difficulty in describing the vision. Most translations, therefore, leave the phrase as it is and let the reader or commentator unfold its possible meanings.

The prophet Ezekiel, earlier than Daniel, also uses the phrase. He is addressed as "son of man" *(ben-'adam)* many times in the course of his book. Here, it seems intended to bring out a *contrast* between him and his angelic guide, and therefore to mean something like "mere man" or "mortal man." The use of *'adam* ("human being," the generic term in Hebrew) as opposed to Daniel's *'enosh* ("male, man" in the gender-specific sense) is probably not significant, but it does prevent us from drawing any conclusions based on the gender of the term.

The phrase did, however, take on a life of its own later, as a general description of the coming of a messianic figure at the end of the era. "The son of man" as a title was less precise than "messiah" (meaning "anointed," as a king was anointed). The royal and political overtones of "messiah" were dangerous in the context of Roman rule, which did not tolerate any vassal-rulers who were not under its control. In addition, "messiah" had come to have overtones that meant restoration of the Davidic kingship and of a politically independent Israel, particularly after the era of the Maccabees (164–64 BCE). It may have been for these reasons that, as it seems, Jesus favored "the son of man" over "messiah" — he applies "son of man" to himself, but only accepts "messiah" as applied to him by others.

But "son of man" was not completely colorless. Over time it had gathered some meanings to itself, and in particular (by the analogy with such Hebraisms as "daughter of Babylon," meaning "Babylon itself") had, among other things, come to convey the idea of "man" in the generic sense: the real man, the full man, *the* Man, the (only) fully human being. This meaning, as applied to Jesus, was possibly also influenced by the "second Adam" imagery in the thought of Paul (see Romans 5.14; 1 Corinthians 15.21–22, 45–49).

The phrase, therefore, now presents problems for the translator. Keeping the Hebraism that has been brought into the Greek of the New Testament — and echoing the usages of Ezekiel and Daniel — can seriously mislead the reader. The phrase in the New Testament does not mean "mere man" or "mortal man" when applied to Jesus, as it does when applied to Ezekiel. Nor does it mean "one resembling a man, but not a man" — that is, an angelic being that looks like (but isn't) a human being — as it does in Daniel 10.16, 18. Even more dangerously, the phrases in Ezekiel and Daniel do not mean "the fully human being, the real Man," and neither one means the kind of messiah that Jesus was. If the translation offers no explanation of this verbal echo, however, there is nothing to stop the uninstructed reader from assimilating Jesus to either of these texts.

In addition, if the New Testament meaning includes the overtones of "real man, fully human being, the second Adam," then "man" in current English usage is no longer adequate. The phrase would need to be translated using much more gender-neutral language in order to avoid conveying the idea that maleness and full humanity are the same thing.

Avoiding "son of man," however, is equally difficult. There is certainly a strong case to be made that the New Testament usage derived from Daniel in particular, and that some of the accoutrements of the mysterious figure that Daniel describes — "I saw one like a human being coming with the clouds of heaven" (7.13, NRSV) — are echoed in Mark 14.62. If the translation obscures that link, the reader or student may never be able to make it.

It is therefore an insoluble problem, and either choice requires some sort of explanation. Versions of the Bible that choose to translate contextually, and therefore avoid "son of man" in one place or another, need to provide literal wording in footnotes (as the NRSV does; see Ezekiel 2.1, Daniel 7.13, translators' notes). Those versions that choose to translate literally may need to offer a "sense" translation in footnotes. Teachers or commentators need to call attention to all of the difficulties attendant on this phrase, and to guard against the easy (and false) identification between the apocalyptic figure in Daniel, who is almost certainly not any sort of human being, and the apocalyptic vision of Jesus, who is.

TORAH

An even more explicit example occurs with the translation of the word *torah* (which is also the title for the first five books of the Bible in Judaism). In Hebrew *torah* is the noun derived from the verb *yrh*, "throw, shoot" (referring variously to shooting an arrow or throwing an object; in Exodus 15.4, the object is the Egyptian army that God has "thrown" or "cast" into the sea). By extension, perhaps either from casting lots as a way of seeking direction or from a gesture used in pointing out the right way to someone, *yrh* came to mean "teach" or "instruct." *Torah,* therefore, means "teaching" or "instruction." It can mean "law," as in Exodus 12.49, where there is "one *torah*" for the stranger and the Israelite, clearly meaning "one standard of judgment, one set of rules to obey." Better, however, and more general in most instances, would be "teaching, instruction," as in Psalm 119.97, "how I love your *torah!*" or Isaiah 51.4, "*torah* will go out from me." "Law," then, would be one particular kind of teaching: not the legal code in itself, but "the law as teacher," that is, the recognition of the cultural fact that ethical behavior can be shaped and influenced by the social precepts and legal requirements of a particular society.

    In Christian translations of the Bible, however, *torah* is generally translated, more or less consistently, as "law." One reason for this was that in the ancient Greek translation of the Hebrew Bible, the Septuagint, *torah* was generally rendered by the Greek word *nomos,* which has a primary meaning of "law." Because the Septuagint became the Bible of the early Christian church — since most Christians could speak or read Greek, while few could read Hebrew — *nomos* became the term in use for the general "instruction" contained in the Bible, and also for the first five books of the Bible — Genesis through Deuteronomy — that were grouped together as "the *torah* of Moses" in both Jewish and Christian terminology. *Nomos* therefore became the title for the entire set of legal prescriptions that Jews accepted as a sign of their commitment to God. Because the sense of the Greek word is narrower than that of the Hebrew word, "law" came to be confined more and more, in the New Testament, to the specific precepts of circumcision, diet, ritual behavior, dress, and so on, that would have marked out the Jews from their surrounding, non-Jewish context. In looking at *torah* in this way, we are clearly not seeing it from within, as a Jew would have experienced it, but from an external viewpoint.

But "law" as a translation of *torah* is still, at best, inadequate. And this is where the translator's difficulties are located. "Law," particularly in the writings of Paul in the New Testament, came to have a specific, restrictive meaning: "law" as opposed to "grace," the effort to obtain righteousness by our own efforts as opposed to the justification, the "making right," that God bestows on us by grace.

There is no doubt that this is a real insight. But it is an insight not into the relationship or contrast between Judaism and Christianity, but into the psychology of human spiritual experience. There exists within most of us, if not all of us, a desire to know the limits of our obligations. We want to know "the rules" so that we can follow them, but also so that we can be done with them. If there is a list, we can check the items off and come to the end of it. "Law," in this sense, means not just our own efforts at "being good," but our wish — even our overmastering desire — to have our obligations defined, and therefore limited.

It is unfortunate, to say the least, that in the New Testament, this spiritual insight was entangled from the first in the dispute between the early Christian community and the Jewish faith from which it had arisen and from which it was gradually separating. Unfortunate, because it has led Christians throughout the centuries since to identify the rigid adherence to a set of (perhaps arbitrary) requirements with Judaism, and the free and humble acceptance of God's grace with Christianity. No doubt there were Jews who rigidly clung to their rules and prescriptions, and who thought that by following them exactly they were discharging their moral obligations. What we must recognize, however, is that they did this not because they were Jewish, but because they were human. And once we recognize this, we can see tendencies to gracious mercy and humility in Judaism as much as in Christianity — and tendencies to legalistic hairsplitting in Christianity at least as much as in Judaism.

When faced with the issue of translating *torah* in the Old Testament of a Christian Bible, therefore, the easy (and misleading) choice is to translate it as "law" so that the New Testament references to "law" are upheld. But within the context of the Hebrew Bible, *torah* should really be rendered as "teaching" or "instruction" in most cases, despite New Testament usage. Although this translation would obscure an important echo in the New Testament of the Hebrew Bible, the fact remains that the translation "law" is inadequate, misleading, and often plain wrong. If necessary, translators' notes can explain the issues involved, but the later text should not be used in this way to dictate a narrower range of meaning for the earlier one.

✼ INCLUSIVE LANGUAGE

WHEN WE TRANSLATE the Bible into English, we are in effect aiming at a moving target, though a slow-moving one: English itself is changing even as we are creating our translations. As any reader of English literature knows, words change in meaning over years and centuries, and usage changes as well. These changes do not always move in one direction; for example, although standards of present-day written English are notably more permissive about "four-letter words" than were the accepted standards in previous centuries, we can sometimes be surprised by the ease with which earlier eras admitted certain words into discourse. In 1 Samuel 25.22, for instance, David (who was not yet king) threatens to kill "every male" (NRSV) in the household of a man who has displeased him. The Hebrew is translated literally in the King James Version as "any that pisseth against the wall" — a translation choice that has not been followed in any modern version (though the Jewish Publication Society's Tanakh includes a slightly different phrasing in a footnote).

Modern English is changing in one way that directly affects translation choices. Increasingly, it is no longer acceptable to use masculine terms — "man," "he," and the like — in ways that imply universal application to both males and females. "Human being," "humanity," and "humankind" have replaced "man" and "mankind"; "he or she" now frequently substitutes for "he" when the reference is general; and, in contemporary Bible translations, "brothers" (Greek *adelphoi*) as a term of address for members of a congregation (see Romans 10.1 and many other places) is rendered "friends" (REB) or "brothers and sisters" (NRSV).

Unfortunately, perhaps because this language change is occurring along with changes in the wider society that affect women's and men's roles, "inclusive language" has become a stand-in for debates on other matters, and a lightning rod for critiques of some modern Bible translations. This issue is also still a contentious one because the changes have occurred within the recent past, and are ongoing, so there are many people alive today for whom older English usage is still the norm. For Bible readers, the King James Version and other older translations — even the Revised Standard Version (1946, 1952, 1971) and the New International Version (1978, 1984) count as "older" on this issue — reflect "non-inclusive" usage that is part of what is changing.

Since this topic has tended to generate more heat than light, we need to step back from it and look at both sides carefully to see where each might have something of value to contribute. And we need to detach this translation issue, as far as possible, from such wider issues as the feminist movement, the effort to include women in all areas of society, and — more specifically for Christians and Jews — the ordination of women. The hardening of positions on many of these other issues has made it more difficult to deal with inclusive language solely in the context of considering how best to translate the Bible.

Finally, we must avoid falling into the trap that some partisans on either side too often do: that of attributing bad motives to those with whom they disagree. For some of those in favor of inclusive language, the opposing group of traditionalists is made up solely of people who are trying to maintain or extend an oppressive patriarchy, and to keep women in subordinate positions and away from any power in society. For some of those who wish to maintain gender-specific language, their opponents who argue in favor of inclusive language are nothing but secular, radical feminists, whose agenda is the destruction of traditional Christianity and of all moral norms in the western tradition. We will instead be looking at both positions solely in terms of how they approach issues of translation and what assumptions they make about conclusions to be drawn on the basis of language choices. And, as will become clear below, we will on these grounds end up criticizing positions taken on both sides, without having to inquire into the motivations of either one.

As part of the effort to treat this subject even-handedly, we will also avoid loaded terms for either side. We will therefore refer to the position of those opposed to the use of inclusive language in translation as "the traditionalist view," rather than as "conservative," "reactionary," and so on. And we will refer to the position of those in favor of inclusive language as "the contemporary view" rather than as "the radical feminist view" or other such phrases.

In order to understand the positions of those involved in this debate, we will try to summarize each one fairly and then look at some specifics of biblical language to see how they may help or hinder us in making translation choices. We will first present the traditionalist view, in a question-and-answer format, and then the contemporary view. Since many different people have made their opinions on this issue known over the past few decades, rather than dealing with the views of specific individuals we will be looking at a summary version of each.

THE TRADITIONALIST VIEW

Question: What, in your view, is the translation issue involved with inclusive language?

Answer: In the view of a traditional approach to the Bible, the matter is simply one of correct and faithful translation. We should not make translation choices based on changes in the secular world; the Bible stands *against* the norms and values of "the world" and should never adopt or reflect them.

Q: But isn't the Bible the product of a particular world-view?

A: The Bible arose in a particular cultural environment, and undoubtedly reflects that, perhaps carrying some limitations of the time and place of its composition — as, for instance, with slavery. But it is not for individual translations or translators to decide what is universal and what is culturally relative, and even on issues where most acknowledge that the Bible's views are inadequate or outdated, the translation should not try to accomplish what an exegete is supposed to do.

Q: What do you mean by "accomplish what an exegete is supposed to do"?

A: In the simplest sense, the translation should not do what a sermon or homily is supposed to do. It should not interpret the text; it should simply present it. If a passage should apply to both men and women, and there is doubt about that fact, the preacher can make that point. If a passage supports the institution of slavery, teachers can acknowledge the change in historical circumstances that has led (correctly and wonderfully) to the abolition of slavery. But in the translation, we cannot erase slavery from the text. The translators must stick to presenting the text as it is.

Q: So you are saying that the issue of masculine privilege in the Bible is the same as the issue of slavery?

A: No, we cannot say that for certain. If the Bible teaches the primacy and priority of the masculine, and if it further teaches that God is male, this may be part of revealed truth. We should not — we dare not — change that in response to aspects of our own culture. To do so is to make an absolute out of our current perceptions, at the expense of the Bible's plain sense.

Q: But what if, as with slavery, the Bible's position is inadequate? What if we eventually come to see that male privilege is a historical accident, and we must move beyond it?

A: That may happen, but if it does, it will happen over many years — perhaps centuries — as did the decision of the Christian community about slavery. We must not short-circuit what should probably be a complex and lengthy negotiation about language, to be tested over many generations and tried out in many differing cultural environments. Only so can we be reasonably sure that we are not simply imposing our own, highly culturally-conditioned view of the masculine and feminine on the text of the Bible.

Q: But then how are we to speak to our current culture, in which the equality of men and women is increasingly taken for granted?

A: The issue of legal equality — of insuring that women are treated fairly, that opportunities in society are open to them as well as to men, and so on — is not something that can be advanced or delayed by a Bible translation. But we must not fall for that recurrent temptation to try to make our faith "relevant" to its "cultured despisers." We will never succeed in bringing such despisers back into the fold of the faithful. When people are converted, they are converted on a deeper level than that of simply finding their current cultural norms validated by their new-found faith. We will not succeed in bringing in those who follow the latest trends, but we may very well succeed in driving the truly faithful out. They will simply not recognize what we are teaching as the traditional faith that they know and love.

Q: Is it true to say, then, that you maintain that God is in fact male?

A: I should rather say that God, while containing both the masculine and feminine, exemplifies the masculine in his interactions with his creation. Therefore, though it should be said that theologically God is "beyond gender," in a personal relationship God has clearly shown that he is to be related to as a masculine being: he is incarnate as a male human being, he is given masculine titles — "King," "Lord," and so on — and he is portrayed through largely masculine imagery. If we accept the idea that we can meet revealed truth through the biblical text, we must accept as a possible part of that idea that our relationship to God is a relationship with a masculine Being. All of this — as part of the revelation we profess to believe in — should be reflected in the language that we use in our Bible translations.

THE CONTEMPORARY VIEW

Q: Why should a Bible translation use gender-inclusive language?

A: As with all other issues in Bible translation, any translation should follow the usage of contemporary English. In current English, there is increasing recognition that we should use gender-inclusive terminology about human beings, because that is the way that the English language is developing. Translations take account of other changes in language. For instance, the King James Version uses "Holy Ghost" (Acts 1.2ff.) whereas modern versions use "Holy Spirit"; the King James Version uses the archaic second-person singular ("thee," "thou," and so on), while in current English we say "you." In the same way, as English usage has changed with regard to gender-inclusive terminology, our translations should change as well.

Q: But isn't this development a somewhat artificial one, driven by a feminist agenda? Why should a translation of the Bible adopt standards from the secular world?

A: I cannot accept your division between the Bible and the "secular" world. For one thing, although it is certainly true that the feminist movement has been among the constituencies pushing gender-neutral or gender-inclusive language, that does not mean it is secular. Many feminists are Christians or Jews; to put it the other way around, many Christians and Jews are feminists, and they regard their religion as supportive of the movement toward gender equality. For another, there is nothing wrong with the religious community in general learning from those outside it: democratic movements, fair labor laws, pure food and drug policies, and many other such progressive and socially-useful efforts arose outside the religious community, or were (at least partly) pushed by groups with a secular agenda; yet I don't think that those of us in the religious community would think these were bad things. In fact, whether they were doing so consciously or not, these groups may have been advancing God's work. Those of us who wish to do God's will often find ourselves working alongside others who are not religious but who have a passion for justice. Inclusive language may simply be one more instance of a place where people of good will can agree on the issue, even if they come to it from different starting points.

Q: But isn't a Bible translation a rather odd place to carry out, or support, a social agenda?

A: The Bible is one of the foundational documents of western civilization. If it maintains a type of language that seems to put maleness in a privileged position, that can send a powerful, discouraging message to women and men who support gender equality. If, on the other hand, it is translated in a way that makes clear the equal dignity of both women and men, that also sends a message, one of empowerment. In our culture, women have for too long been regarded as unable to represent the fullness of humanity, whereas men have always been seen to do so. "He" has traditionally included "she," and "man" has included "woman," in a way that was not true of the inverse: "all women are mortal" would not have sounded the same as "all men are mortal." The weight of this linguistic legacy must be counteracted, among other places, in translations of the Bible, so that any general reference to human beings should be couched in language that is gender-neutral. Instead of "man" one should say "human being" or "humankind." Instead of "he" one should say "he or she" or, casting whole sentences into the plural form, "they." When it is translated in this way, the Bible can make a powerful statement about gender equality.

Q: I think many people would agree with you about language referring to human beings. But you also want to change the language about God. How do you justify that?

A: I know that gender-inclusive God-language makes many people uncomfortable. They think it is changing not just language but our thought about the nature of God. But think for a moment. God, who is beyond gender, and in whose image both male and female were created, should not be referred to as if God were male. Otherwise, we are in danger of elevating maleness to an intrinsic characteristic of divinity. That limits God, and we then find ourselves worshiping a god who is less than God. That is idolatrous. If our translation can help to guard against such an error, more power to it. We therefore argue that God should not be referred to by the pronoun "he," that God should be "ruler," not "king," and so on. In doing so, incidentally, we also think we are being truer to the Bible itself, which uses feminine imagery for God (see Isaiah 42.14, which compares God to a woman in labor) and Jesus (see Matthew 23.37, in which Jesus compares himself to a hen gathering her chicks under her wings). By translating carefully, in such a way as to minimize the masculine references to God and to balance them where we can with feminine language, we will be helping people to see that God includes all aspects of reality, including the reality we experience as gender. And that will also help everyone to see that women can express and represent God as much as men.

CAN WE BRIDGE THE GULF?

There may seem to be such a gulf between these positions that it appears there is no common ground left. We can, however, look at some of the issues that each side has raised, to see whether they can shed any light on the matter.

Must we accept patriarchy as revealed truth?

The Bible is most certainly the product of some very patriarchal cultures. No translation can remove that fact. When, however, we examine the nature of the patriarchal values that some passages in the Bible exemplify, it might cause us to wonder whether we should so easily accept the masculine language that also characterizes the Bible. It does, in other words, put the issue of gender-exclusive language in sharper perspective, and make it much harder to argue that a patriarchal stance is a part of revealed truth, to which we must simply conform.

Most present-day Christians and Jews would not endorse the Bible's view of certain aspects of the relationship between males and females. Take, for instance, this passage from Deuteronomy:

> If a man meets a virgin who is not engaged [i.e., to marry someone else], and seizes her and lies with her, and they are caught in the act, the man who lay with her shall give fifty shekels of silver to the young woman's father, and she shall become his wife. (22.28–29, NRSV)

This is not a matter of translation approach. It should be clear that no one — no traditionalist, any more than any adherent to contemporary views about the relations between men and women — could defend an approach to violent sexual crime based on this passage. Note that the presumption of the passage is that the rape is primarily an injury to the rape victim's father, not to the woman herself. Note also that besides the monetary penalty exacted from the rapist — the payment of a bride price to the father, in recompense for having destroyed his daughter's value — the "punishment" of the rapist consists in having him marry his victim. No modern penal code would dare to incorporate such an approach to the punishment for rape.

Clearly, in the matter of gender relations, we are all at some distance from at least some of the Bible's prescriptions. And once we have seen that we cannot adopt the Bible's point of view on such a matter, it is certainly legitimate to ask whether we must accept the Bible's gender-specific language as a part of its intrinsic content, which must be reflected in a translation.

Do traditional translations ever use "gender-inclusive" language?

Despite what we may assume, it is not the case that "inclusive" translation approaches are a merely modern phenomenon. Take a verse from the Beatitudes, Matthew 5.9: "Blessed are the peacemakers, for they shall be called the *huioi* of God." In six traditional English translations of the Bible, from Tyndale (1525) through the King James Version (1611), and including the Rheims edition prepared by Roman Catholics, the Greek word was translated "children." In 1881, however, with the British

Revised Version, and continuing through the American Revised Standard Version (1946), the word was translated "sons."

There is no doubt that, lexically speaking, *huios* has a primary meaning of "male child," and that there are different words — *pais* and *teknon* — for "child." The word *huios* also carries the meaning of "the one who will inherit," since sons were the heirs of their fathers. The passage uses *huioi* (plural of *huios*), so what translation is appropriate?

The older translations clearly opted for a word that conveyed what they took to be the real meaning of the statement: "children." Should the translation limit the meaning of the verse, in conformity with the lexical choice, to "male offspring"? Can we conclude that only males can be peacemakers, or that women who are peacemakers are deemed to be male offspring of God? Or should we rather, with the traditional English translations, agree that the real meaning of the passage applies to everyone, male or female, and "sons" is therefore a misleading rendering?

Can we rely on gender choices in the original language?

An indication that we cannot necessarily rely on the biblical writers to be completely consistent on matters of lexical gender indicators comes in a passage having to do with the arrangements for the Last Supper before Jesus' betrayal and crucifixion. Jesus arranges a final meal with his followers. Clearly, he knows that it is likely his enemies will be alerted to his whereabouts in Jerusalem, and he wants to have his meal with his friends without interruption. In order to avoid a betrayal in advance, he does not tell them where to meet; instead, to prevent any one of them from giving out the information, he arranges for them to be conducted to the place where the supper is to be held.

In both Mark and Luke, the gospel writers say that he tells them to look for an *anthropos* carrying a jar of water (Mark 14.13; Luke 22.10). *Anthropos* is the Greek word meaning "human being" in the general sense; *aner/andros* and *gyne/gynaikos* are the words for "male person" and "female person" respectively. Yet here, *anthropos* clearly must mean "male person." The reason is that carrying water was a woman's task. If the gospel writers had meant to convey that Jesus had said to his followers, "Go follow *a person* who is carrying a jar of water," the instruction would have made no sense. Any number of persons — all of them women — could have been carrying water that evening. The distinctive thing that the disciples were to be looking for was *a male person* carrying a jar of water. Thus, even though *anthropos* is not the primary term for "male person," here the gospel writers are using it in that sense.

Is traditional English usage clear-cut?

"Man" in English, even for those who maintain its traditional sense as meaning "inclusively human" (depending upon context), still has overtones of masculinity. This is most clearly seen in contexts where the term comes up against aspects of humanity characteristic of females rather than males. The test-case sentence has come to be the following: "Man, like all mammals, breastfeeds his young." It is very difficult to read or hear that sentence without coming up against the dissonance between the supposed universality of "man" and "his" and the actuality that they are masculine forms — in fact, it is impossible to hear or read the sentence without recognizing that it is objectively false.

Must we maintain the gender choices of the underlying languages?

To demand without nuance that translations must follow the gender choices of the original biblical languages is to mandate that one translation approach — the formal, "word-for-word" rendering — is the only legitimate one. As the argument of this book should have made clear by now, that is not a tenable approach. If carried to an extreme, such a philosophy of translation would require too slavish a rendering in many places. (For an example of what happens in general when a translation slavishly follows the style of the original language, see the fairly literal translation of a narrative from the fifth chapter of Mark below, pp. 74–75.) In addition, the argument that we must reproduce all gendered language exactly as it is in the original text misunderstands the nature of lexical gender (see the discussion below, pp. 50–54).

Can "inclusive" translation ever be misleading?

Efforts to render the Bible in inclusive language can occasionally lead to misleading renderings, and this is something that must be taken into account. In the New Revised Standard Version, there is a very commendable effort to make it clear that much of biblical prayer is applicable to human beings in general. In the Psalms, therefore, where the original text has "man" (Hebrew 'ish), the New Revised Standard Version often translates by putting everything into the third-person plural ("those... they"), since unlike the third-person singular form in English, the plural form is gender-neutral.

But this practice has led the New Revised Standard Version translators astray in one passage in which a New Testament writer, the author of the letter to the Hebrews, quotes a psalm. As a part of the argument that Jesus Christ fulfills what was latent in the Hebrew Bible, the author of this letter quotes Psalm 8.4–6. In the NRSV, however, Psalm 8 has been translated from Hebrew in gender-inclusive terms, meaning that the terms "man" ('enosh) and "son of man" (ben-'adam) have been translated "human beings" and "mortals" respectively.

As a rendering of the Hebrew this is perfectly defensible. But in context in Hebrews, where the writer of the letter clearly intends the reader to understand these references as being specifically to Jesus Christ, the translation should have rendered the Greek text literally, instead of adapting it to the NRSV rendition of the Hebrew. It is necessary to read the NRSV footnotes to understand what the text is trying to get across. The NRSV text says:

> Now God did not subject the coming world, about which we
> are speaking, to angels. But someone has testified somewhere,
>> "What are human beings that you are mindful of them,
>> or mortals, that you care for them?
>> You have made them for a little while lower than the angels;
>> you have crowned them with glory and honor,
>> subjecting all things under their feet." (Hebrews 2.5–8)

In the Greek text, the psalm quotation reads as follows:

"What is man that you are mindful of him,
  or the son of man, that you care for him?
You have made him for a little while lower than the angels;
  you have crowned him with glory and honor,
  subjecting all things under his feet."

The New Revised Standard Version is to be commended for including translators' notes that make clear what it has done in this passage. But it would have been better — clearer, and also better translation — to have left the translation of the Greek as literal as possible, in order to make the writer's point clear. It is also necessary, however, to point out the discrepancies between the original meaning of the psalm and its use in Hebrews: for example, in order to make the point, the writer of Hebrews changed "a little lower than the angels" (meaning that human beings are, in fact, not divine or heavenly creatures) to "for a little while lower than the angels" (meaning that Jesus as messiah is in reality *above* the angels, although he submitted to being below them for a time). In other words, good translation will take seriously *both* what the writer of Hebrews says *and* what the writer of Psalm 8 says, without subordinating either one to the other.

THE CURRENT STATE OF THE DEBATE

In recent years, when inclusive language translations have been published, those favoring traditional language have attacked them as illegitimate approaches to the biblical text. The substantive attacks — leaving aside critiques that these translations are carrying out a radical feminist agenda that is anti-Christian, a criticism which does not address translation issues — are primarily of two sorts: that messianic prophecies in the Old Testament are obscured by inclusive language approaches, and that translations should try to reproduce the gender-specific language of the original texts because that is a part of the inspired literature that we must accept if we are in the community of faith.

We looked at one example of preserving messianic language in chapter 4 in the section dealing with the phrase "son of man" (pp. 31ff.), and we discussed another example just above, regarding the translation of Psalm 8 quoted in the letter to the Hebrews. In the first case, as we explained, there are problems for the translators no matter what approach — word-for-word or meaning-for-meaning — they adopt. In the second case, we showed that it is better to translate literally, because the writer of the letter to the Hebrews is using the psalm to make a point about Jesus, but it is also necessary to call attention to the writer's adjustment of the language of the psalm in order to support the point — an adjustment that misreads what the psalm is saying.

The issue of lexical gender is another matter. Like many world languages, but unlike modern English, Hebrew and Greek use lexical gender; that is, nouns in both languages have a gender, masculine or feminine, or, in the case of Greek, neuter. So, for instance, the word for "God" in Hebrew *('elohim)* is masculine; Greek offers two forms, *theos* (male god) and *thea* (female god). Such words take verbs to match their gender, so that "God" takes verbs such as "he created," "he was," and so on. But so do ordinary nouns, like "stone" (Hebrew *'eben*, Greek *lithos*). When we translate these nouns, we say "it" rather than "he," following English usage. In Genesis 31.45, for example, we have: "Jacob took a stone, and set it up as a pillar"; he did not "set him up." In the same way, if we decided to translate the Bible, for theological reasons, in such a way as to eliminate any pronouns for God, the fact that such pronouns (and their associated verbs) in Hebrew and Greek are masculine would not make any difference in English. As a counter-example, the Hebrew word for "spirit" or "breath" *(ruach)* is feminine, but we ordinarily do not translate it with feminine pronouns. In Numbers 11.17, 25, for example, the Lord takes "the spirit that is on" Moses and puts "it" — not "her" — on the elders.

Abstract nouns are sometimes personified, and the most prominent one in the biblical text is "wisdom," which in both Hebrew *(chokhmah)* and Greek *(sophia)* is feminine. Thus in the book of Proverbs wisdom *(chokhmah)* speaks and, being treated as in effect a person, she is referred to by feminine pronouns:

> Does not wisdom cry out,
> And understanding lift up her voice?
> She takes her stand on the top of the high hill,
> Beside the way, where the paths meet.
> She cries out by the gates, at the entry of the city,
> At the entrance of the doors.... (8:1–3, NKJV)

Similarly, in the Wisdom of Jesus ben Sirach (Ecclesiasticus) (24.1–2), wisdom *(sophia)* is called "she":

> Wisdom shall praise her own self, and shall be honoured in
> God, and shall glory in the midst of her people,
> And shall open her mouth in the churches of the most High,
> and shall glorify herself in the sight of his power.... (Douay)

Finally, in the Wisdom of Solomon, wisdom *(sophia)* is again "she." In this last passage particularly, Wisdom takes on quasi-divine attributes, and it became an influence on the Christian doctrine of the creative Logos:

> I learned both what is secret and what is manifest,
> for wisdom, the fashioner of all things, taught me.
> There is in her a spirit that is intelligent, holy,
> unique, manifold, subtle,
> mobile, clear, unpolluted,
> distinct, invulnerable, loving the good, keen,
> irresistible, beneficent, humane,
> steadfast, sure, free from anxiety,
> all-powerful, overseeing all,
> and penetrating through all spirits
> that are intelligent, pure, and altogether subtle.
> For wisdom is more mobile than any motion;
> because of her pureness she pervades and
>   penetrates all things.
> For she is a breath of the power of God,
> and a pure emanation of the glory of the Almighty;
> therefore nothing defiled gains entrance into her.
> For she is a reflection of eternal light,

a spotless mirror of the working of God,
and an image of his goodness.
Although she is but one, she can do all things,
and while remaining in herself, she renews all things;
in every generation she passes into holy souls
and makes them friends of God, and prophets;
for God loves nothing so much as the person
   who lives with wisdom.
She is more beautiful than the sun,
and excels every constellation of the stars.
Compared with the light she is found to be superior,
for it is succeeded by the night,
but against wisdom evil does not prevail.
She reaches mightily from one end of the earth to the other,
and she orders all things well. (7.21–8.1, NRSV)

Compare this with the unfolding of the mystery of the *logos* (a masculine noun often translated using masculine pronouns) in the prologue to the Gospel of John (1.1–14), or with this passage in Colossians dealing with the cosmic Christ:

He is the image of the invisible God, the firstborn of all creation; for in [*or* "by"] him all things in heaven and on earth were created, things visible and invisible, whether thrones or dominions or rulers or powers — all things have been created through him and for him. He himself is before all things, and in [*or* "by"] him all things hold together. He is the head of the body, the church; he is the beginning, the firstborn from the dead, so that he might come to have first place in everything. For in him all the fullness of God was pleased to dwell, and through him God was pleased to reconcile to himself all things, whether on earth or in heaven, by making peace through the blood of his cross. (1:15–20, NRSV)

Are we justified, then, in taking this fact of lexical gender and drawing a theological conclusion from it? Suppose we argue as follows: (1) Wisdom in the book of the Wisdom of Solomon is the principle of order and creation in the universe; (2) in the Christian understanding this role is played by the *logos* (John 1.3–4, 10); and (3) in Colossians 1.15–20 Christ is portrayed as the agent of creation, in whom all things hold together, in a way similar to Wisdom in the earlier passage. Therefore, a feminine principle is at the basis of the creative *logos,* and the Word is in fact "she."

I do not think we can argue in this way. If we do so, we are building a central theological understanding on a very weak basis. But it is important to understand that if we reject this argument as invalid, we must also reject any argument about the "maleness" of God based on the lexical gender of the words used in the biblical text. In fact, we should, on the same grounds, argue that the use of masculine pronouns to translate *logos* in the prologue to John is also incorrect ("*He* was in the beginning.... All things came into being through *him...* " [1.2–3]). This is not a matter of accurately reflecting the gender of Jesus of Nazareth. Jesus was male, it is true; but even if we fully accept that Jesus was also the incarnate Word, Jesus' maleness does not have any effect on whether God is masculine. The *logos* is divine; no matter how high our Christology is, we cannot work backwards from the incarnation into the humanly masculine Jesus of the lexically masculine *logos* or of the *phos* ("light") in John 1.9ff. to assert that divinity is masculine.

I wish to be as clear as possible here. In English, neuter pronouns are not ordinarily used for persons; "it" means an object, not someone with whom we can have a personal relationship. *If we use pronouns at all* for persons, they must, in English, be gendered to express personhood. So the *logos* or the cosmic Christ, in a traditional translation, can be "he." But if we wish to translate without creating the incorrect implication that we are asserting masculinity of Godhood, we will simply have to repeat the titles, "Word" or "Christ," rather than use pronouns, or say "that one" or "the same" or words to that effect.

Finally, what about the image of "Father"? Jesus used this word to describe his relationship to God; does it not indicate that God is male? Once again, I think we cannot argue in this way. The difficulty in finding an alternative translation for "Father" is one that a theologian would have to face in any argument about the gender of God. The point of the language, however, is to emphasize the intimacy of the relationship between Jesus and the Father, not to make a point about God's gender.

(The word Jesus used, *Abba,* is a child's word, an informal term.) Once again, I do not think we can draw a theological conclusion from a lexical fact.

FULLY INCLUSIVE TRANSLATION

From all of this disparate material, I think we can come to a few decisions. First, with regard to standard translation, there are clearly things to be said in favor of accommodating the less extreme views on both sides — things in favor of moderate changes in language that will recognize the changes in English usage over the past few decades, and things in favor of conserving traditional language where that is appropriate. We cannot return to the days of "man/men" as generic nouns, meaning "human beings in general" or "men and women"; nor can we say that "he" means "he and she" or that "brothers" means "brothers and sisters." We must translate in such a way that when the reference is to the generality of human beings, the text makes that clear.

Second, neither the original language texts nor the history of English provide unambiguous support for either side in the debate. The ancient writers did not have our concerns, and therefore they did not make the kinds of choices, in either direction, that we would have liked them to make. We must find our own way in this matter.

Finally, whatever the hopes and fears might be on either side, it is certainly the case now that there is no single, definitive translation of the Bible. The King James Version, and such other traditional translations as the New International Version, the Revised Standard Version, and the New King James Version, will exist alongside more modern, more gender-inclusive renderings. Since that is the case, why should there not be one choice that is completely inclusive in all of its translation choices? We have seen above that lexical facts, either in favor of feminine language about God or in favor of retaining traditional masculine language, cannot be used to draw theological conclusions. For that very reason, therefore, it would be valuable to have a translation that refused to reflect any of those lexical facts: one in which God, angels, the risen Christ, and even Satan were not gendered beings but clearly existed in a realm that was "beyond gender." For those who would not like such a translation, many other choices exist and will continue to exist. Right now, there is no readily available rendering that offers the opposite choice. For all of those who wish to experience the widest range of translation possibilities, it would be of great benefit for some group to agree to weather the inevitable criticism and undertake such a project.

Chapter 6

⚜ SOME SPECIFIC EXAMPLES IN BIBLE TRANSLATIONS

NOW THAT WE have looked at a number of translation issues and problems in general, and at translation of the Bible in particular, we can look at some specific examples of the decisions that various translators have made, and why they have made them. In some cases we can look at one passage to see how it has handled a particular translation problem, and in others we can compare different translations to make the point as clearly as possible.

INTERLINEAR TRANSLATION

An interlinear translation — one that follows the exact wording and structure of the underlying source language — shows what the formal equivalent approach would be like if there were no constraints on its use of the target language, English. For this extract I have used a very familiar text from Matthew's gospel, the Lord's Prayer. The rendering follows the exact word-order of the Greek text, using hyphens to show where one word in the Greek has to be represented by two English words. It also leaves out words ("are" in the first line, for instance) that are understood in Greek but should be included in idiomatic English, and it includes words ("the" in the last line) that are present in the Greek but would ordinarily be omitted in English.

> Father of-us who in the heavens,
> be holy the name of-you;
> come the kingdom of-you;
> become the will of-you as in heaven and upon earth;
> the bread of-us the necessary give to-us today;
> and remit to-us the debts of-us,
> as also we remit the indebted-ones of-us;
> and not bring-in us into trial,
> but deliver us from the evil. (Matthew 6.9–13)

It is clear that some meaning could be puzzled out from this, but it should also be clear that a translation carried out along these lines would not be read. It is not really English, and shows the extreme case of taking the source language as the overriding, controlling factor of the translation, while leaving English to fend for itself.

HIGHLY FORMAL TRANSLATION

The following rendition of the opening of Genesis (1.1–13) is about as literal a translation as one could render that is still readable as English: the Everett Fox translation of the Hebrew Bible. Note the repetitions ("sprout forth with sprouting-growth," "seed forth seeds") that represent the different forms of the same word in the underlying Hebrew. The Fox translation gives us a good sense of how the Hebrew works, but it does not "represent" the experience of reading the Hebrew text for anyone in the original audience. What sounds exotic to us, because of the compounding of words, the verbal echoes, and the unusual sentence structure, would not have seemed so to an ancient Hebrew-speaker.

> At the beginning of God's creating
> of the heavens and the earth,
> when the earth was wild and waste,
> darkness over the face of Ocean,
> rushing-spirit of God hovering over the face of the waters —

God said: Let there be light! And there was light.
God saw the light: that it was good.
God separated the light from the darkness.
God called the light: Day! and the darkness he called: Night!
There was setting, there was dawning: one day.

God said:
Let there be a dome amid the waters,
and let it separate waters from waters!
God made the dome
and separated the waters that were below the dome
   from the waters that were above the dome.
It was so.
God called the dome: Heaven!
There was setting, there was dawning: second day.

God said:
Let the waters under the heavens be gathered to one place,
and let the dry land be seen!
It was so.
God called the dry land: Earth!
and the gathering of the waters he called: Seas!
God saw that it was good.
God said:
Let the earth sprout forth with sprouting-growth,
plants that seed forth seeds, fruit trees that yield fruit, after
   their kind, (and) in which is their seed, upon the earth!
It was so.
The earth brought forth sprouting-growth,
plants that seed forth seeds, after their kind,
trees that yield fruit, in which is their seed, after their kind.
God saw that it was good.
There was setting, there was dawning: third day.

A COMPARISON OF TRANSLATIONS
FOR GENESIS 1.1-5

Nine different renderings of the opening of Genesis (1.1-5) demonstrate how even relatively middle-of-the-road translations, as well as some that are closer to being paraphrases, can differ on issues of English rendering.

In the beginning God created the heavens and the earth. The earth was without form and void, and darkness was upon the face of the deep; and the Spirit of God was moving over the face of the waters.

And God said, "Let there be light"; and there was light. And God saw that the light was good; and God separated the light from the darkness. God called the light Day, and the darkness he called Night. And there was evening and there was morning, one day. (RSV)

In the beginning when God created the heavens and the earth, the earth was a formless void and darkness covered the face of the deep, while a wind from God swept over the face of the waters. Then God said, "Let there be light"; and there was light. And God saw that the light was good; and God separated the light from the darkness. God called the light Day, and the darkness he called Night. And there was evening and there was morning, the first day. (NRSV)

In the beginning God created the heavens and the earth. The earth was a vast waste, darkness covered the deep, and the spirit of God hovered over the surface of the water. God said, "Let there be light," and there was light; and God saw the light was good, and he separated light from darkness. He called the light day, and the darkness night. So evening came, and morning came; it was the first day. (REB)

In the beginning, when God created the heavens and the earth, the earth was a formless wasteland, and darkness covered the abyss, while a mighty wind swept over the waters.

Then God said, "Let there be light," and there was light. God saw how good the light was. God then separated the light from the darkness. God called the light "day," and the darkness he called "night." Thus evening came, and morning followed — the first day. (NAB)

In the beginning God created heaven and earth. Now the earth was a formless void, there was darkness over the deep, with a divine wind sweeping over the waters.

God said, 'Let there be light,' and there was light. God saw that light was good, and God divided light from darkness. God called light 'day,' and darkness he called 'night.' Evening came and morning came: the first day. (NJB)

In the beginning of creation, when God made heaven and earth, the earth was without form and void, with darkness over the face of the abyss, and a mighty wind that swept over the surface of the waters. God said, 'Let there be light', and there was light; and God saw that the light was good, and he separated light from darkness. He called the light day, and the darkness night. So evening came, and morning came, the first day. (NEB)

When God began to create heaven and earth — the earth being unformed and void, with darkness over the surface of the deep and a wind from God sweeping over the water — God said, "Let there be light"; and there was light. God saw that the light was good, and God separated the light from the darkness. God called the light Day, and the darkness He called Night. And there was evening and there was morning, a first day. (NJPS)

When God began to create heaven and earth, and the earth then was welter and waste and darkness over the deep and God's breath hovering over the waters, God said, "Let there be light." And there was light. And God saw the light, that it was good, and God divided the light from the darkness. And God called the light Day, and the darkness He called Night. And it was evening and it was morning, first day. (Alter)

First this: God created the Heavens and Earth — all you see, all you don't see. Earth was a soup of nothingness, a bottomless

emptiness, an inky blackness. God's Spirit brooded like a bird
above the watery abyss.
  God spoke:"Light!"
    And light appeared.
  God saw that light was good
    And separated light from dark.
  God named the light Day,
    he named the dark Night.
  It was evening, it was morning —
  Day One. (The Message)

Three matters are of particular interest when we compare
these different approaches. The first matter is the very opening
phrase: should it be "In the beginning God created" or should it
be "When God began to create"? Hebrew does not have many
ways of subordinating clauses, and so the question partly turns
on what the passage is actually saying. The traditional translation — "In the beginning... " — conveys the doctrinal idea that
God created everything. Most scholars now maintain that, whatever we think doctrinally, this is not what the passage means.
Instead, it says, "God worked with formless stuff." The older
translation was influenced by the doctrine of *creatio ex nihilo,*
the later philosophical idea that God created "from nothing,"
not from some preexisting matter that God shaped into the
world as we know it. This is good theology, but it is not good
translation.

The second issue that arises in translations of this passage is
the one of how to represent the phrase that the Revised
Standard Version renders "without form and void": *tohu we-
bohu* ("toe-HOO wuh-boe-HOO") in Hebrew. This is an obscure
phrase because the second word in it — *bohu* — occurs only
in this combination. For instance, in Jeremiah 4.23, the prophet
says, "I looked on the earth, and lo, it was *waste and void...* "
(NRSV). The first word in this composite phrase, the word *tohu,*
in other contexts means "the wilderness, the wasteland" outside
settled areas. For example, Deuteronomy 32.10 reads: "He found
him in a desert region,/ In an empty howling *waste.*" Here *tohu*
is parallel to the general Hebrew word for "desert" or "wilderness," *midbar.* The general sense of the phrase is clear enough

— "empty, chaotic" — but it is not known if *bohu* is a genuine word with a meaning of its own, or only a rhyming word that serves to emphasize and repeat the first word. Alter has represented the Hebrew verbal pattern of rhyme with the English pattern of alliteration: "welter and waste." The Message has taken the approach of repetition and represented it in meaning, translating the one Hebrew phrase using three English phrases, each trying to express something that is formless — soup, bottomless, inky — combined with something that is empty — nothingness, emptiness, blackness.

The third matter is the approach that each version takes to translating the Hebrew word *ruach*. This word — like Greek *pneuma* or Latin *spiritus* — can mean both "spirit" and "breath" or "wind." Some have chosen "wind," and two — the New English Bible and the New American Bible — have even dropped the term "God" in favor of "mighty wind." Only Alter chose "breath." Others chose "spirit," and two — the Revised Standard Version and The Message — have further capitalized "Spirit" as a way of emphasizing divinity (and perhaps covertly introducing the Christian concept of a Trinitarian God).

A COMPARISON OF THE BEGINNING OF THE GOSPEL OF JOHN (1.1-5)

Nine versions of the opening of the Gospel of John (1.1-5) show a variety of approaches to that classic text.

> In the beginning was the Word, and the Word was with God, and the Word was God. He was in the beginning with God; all things were made through him, and without him was not anything made that was made. In him was life, and the life was the light of men. The light shines in the darkness, and the darkness has not **overcome** it. (RSV)

> In the beginning was the Word, and the Word was with God, and the Word was God. He was with God in the beginning.
> Through him all things were made; without him nothing was made that has been made. In him was life, and that life was the

light of men. The light shines in the darkness, but the darkness has not **understood** it. (NIV)

In the beginning was the Word:
the Word was with God
and the Word was God.
He was with God in the beginning.
Through him all things came into being,
not one thing came into being except through him.
What has come into being in him was life,
life that was the light of men;
and light shines in darkness,
and darkness could not **overpower** it. (NJB)

In the beginning the Word already existed.
  The Word was with God,
  and the Word was God.
He existed in the beginning with God.
God created everything through him,
  and nothing was created except through him.
The Word gave life to everything that was created,
  and his life brought light to everyone.
The light shines in the darkness,
  and the darkness can never **extinguish** it. (NLT)

The Logos existed in the very beginning,
the Logos was with God,
the Logos was divine.
He was with God in the very beginning:
through him all existence came into being,
no existence came into being apart from him.
In him life lay,
and this life was the Light for men:
amid the darkness the Light shone,
but the darkness did not **master** it. (Moffatt)

Before the world was created, the Word already existed; he was with God, and he was the same as God. From the very beginning, the Word was with God. Through him God made all things; not one thing in all creation was made without him. The Word was the source of life, and this life brought light to men. The light shines in the darkness, and the darkness has never **put it out.** (TEV)

In the beginning was the one
   who is called the Word.
The Word was with God
   and was truly God.
From the very beginning
   the Word was with God.

And with this Word,
   God created all things.
Nothing was made
   without the Word.
Everything that was created
   received its life from him,
and his life gave light
   to everyone.
The light keeps shining
   in the dark,
and darkness has never
   put it out. (CEV)

The Word was first,
   the Word present to God,
   God present to the Word.
The Word was God,
   in readiness for God from day one.

Everything was created through him;
   nothing — not one thing! —
   came into being without him.
What came into existence was Life,
   and the Life was Light to live by.
The Life-Light blazed out of the darkness;
   the darkness couldn't **put it out.** (The Message)

> At the beginning God expressed himself. That personal expression, that word, was with God, and was God, and he existed with God from the beginning. All creation took place through him, and none took place without him. In him appeared life and this life was the light of mankind. The light still shines in the darkness and the darkness has never **put it out**. (Phillips)

The most obvious characteristic when these translations are displayed in this way is that some of them treat the passage as prose, some as poetry. (Although there are balanced phrases in the original, it does not seem to have the accentual structure of classical Greek poetry.) Those translations that print this passage in poetic form are perhaps indicating that it might have been an early Christian hymn.

Note particularly the translation of the Greek word *logos* — usually represented in English as "Word" — in these versions. *Logos* does mean "something uttered," and in that sense "word," but its range is much broader. It is the expression of a reasoning being, not simply a grunt or an exclamation. James Moffatt, in his translation, simply does not translate it at all and leaves the reader to supply a meaning. In doing so, of course, Moffatt is relying on a general familiarity with the passage; otherwise, the translation would make no sense. Leaving the word untranslated in this way is in effect to say, "You know that this means (roughly) 'word,' but it really means more than that and you should think about this wider meaning when you read this passage."

Phillips (the last example) takes a different approach, and one that is only partly successful. He does not translate the first occurrence of the term, but tries to paraphrase its meaning. He was unfortunate in selecting a phrase that has come to mean a particular, even idiosyncratic, effusion of one's particular "take" on things — "self-expression." In addition, he does not get in the rational aspect of *logos,* the aspect of it that makes it the root of "logical" and all of the "-logy" words in English that mean "study of."

Another translation difficulty in this passage comes with the verb *katalambano* (*katelaben* in the text — a past tense). The English renderings of this word are in boldface type. This verb means "to take (as in the hand) in such a way as to hold firmly or fully." By extension it means "to understand, comprehend." A similar overlapping meaning occurs in English with the verb "grasp," which can mean both "hold physically" and "understand." In the final phrase of this extract, "the light shines in the darkness, but the darkness has not *katelaben* it," there is a classic translator's dilemma. The writer probably meant both "hold so as to extinguish" and "understand the nature of" — the darkness has not extinguished the light, and the darkness has not understood the real nature of the light. In English, however, it is not possible to convey both of these meanings at once, and therefore it is necessary to choose.

AN EXAMPLE OF SYNTACTICAL CORRESPONDENCE: ROMANS 1.1-7

The following excerpts from Romans (1.1-7) show the consequences of trying to reproduce Greek sentence structure in English, versus the choice of rendering the same passage into a number of English sentences with much simplified syntactical structure. These first seven verses of Romans are one long sentence, with numerous clauses, in Greek.

> Paul, a servant of Jesus Christ, called *to be* an apostle, separated unto the gospel of God, (which he had promised afore by his prophets in the holy scriptures,) concerning his son Jesus Christ our Lord, which was made of the seed of David according to the flesh; and declared *to be* the Son of God with power, according to the spirit of holiness, by the resurrection from the dead: by whom we have received grace and apostleship, for obedience to the faith among all nations, for his name: among whom are ye also the called of Jesus Christ: to all that be in Rome, beloved of God, called *to be* saints: Grace to you and peace from God our Father, and the Lord Jesus Christ. (KJV; one sentence)

> Paul, a bond-servant of Christ Jesus, called *as* an apostle, set apart for the gospel of God, which He promised beforehand through His prophets in the holy Scriptures, concerning His

Son, who was born of the seed of David according to the flesh, who was declared with power *to be* the Son of God by [*or* "as a result of"] the resurrection from the dead, according to the Spirit of holiness, Jesus Christ our Lord, through whom we have received grace and apostleship to bring about *the* obedience of faith among all the Gentiles for His name's sake, among whom you also are the called of Jesus Christ; to all who are beloved of God in Rome, called *as* saints: Grace to you and peace from God our Father and the Lord Jesus Christ. (NASB; one sentence)

Other versions translate this single Greek sentence into a number of short English sentences:

From Paul, a servant of Christ Jesus. God called me to be an apostle and chose me to tell the Good News.

God promised this Good News long ago through his prophets, as it is written in the Holy Scriptures. The Good News is about God's Son, Jesus Christ our Lord. As a man, he was born from the family of David. But through the Spirit of holiness he was appointed to be God's Son with great power by rising from the dead. Through Christ, God gave me the special work of an apostle, which was to lead people of all nations to believe and obey. I do this work for him. And you who are in Rome are also called to belong to Jesus Christ.

To all of you in Rome whom God loves and has called to be his holy people:

Grace and peace to you from God our Father and the Lord Jesus Christ. (NCV; 10 sentences)

I, Paul, am a devoted slave of Jesus Christ on assignment, authorized as an apostle to proclaim God's words and acts. I write this letter to all the Christians in Rome, God's friends.

The sacred writings contain preliminary reports by the prophets on God's Son. His descent from David roots him in history; his unique identity as Son of God was shown by the Spirit when Jesus was raised from the dead, setting him apart as the Messiah, our Master. Through him we received both the generous gift of his life and the urgent task of passing it on to others who receive it by entering into obedient trust in Jesus. You are who you are through this gift and call of Jesus Christ! And I greet you now with all the generosity of God our Father and our Master Jesus, the Messiah. (The Message; 7 sentences)

The King James Version and the New American Standard Bible both reproduce this single sentence, giving a rather breathless effect and also making it necessary to parse the sentence in order to understand what goes with what. Note, for instance, that the King James Version has conceded something to English sentence structure by moving "Jesus Christ our Lord" to follow "his son," whereas the New American Standard has left the division between the phrases in place as it is in the Greek original, separated by the long series of clauses "who was born... holiness." It is necessary to read the New American Standard Bible rendition carefully to understand that "Jesus Christ our Lord" is not equated with "the Spirit of holiness" but with "His Son." Comparison of these two versions with the more idiomatic ones in the New Century Version and The Message shows that translations aiming at syntactical correspondence almost inevitably are at a higher reading level than those that are more idiomatic.

LEXICAL CONSISTENCY AND CONTEXTUAL RENDERING: EPHESIANS 1.3

Lexical consistency is compared to contextual rendering in these next extracts, from Ephesians 1.3. In the original Greek verse (which is the beginning of a lengthy sentence), three words — *eulogetos, eulogesas,* and *eulogia* — are different forms of the same root, "bless." This kind of verbal echo was considered good Greek style, but in English it tends to sound redundant, and therefore writers in English use varying vocabulary rather than echoes of the same word. Traditional and formal translations of Ephesians reproduce the effect of the Greek style, whereas more contemporary, freer translations do not. In one case, however — that of The Message — a very free approach to sentence structure is combined with a strict adherence to lexical consistency.

Blessed be the God and Father of our Lord Jesus Christ, who hath blessed us with spiritual blessings in heavenly *places*.... (Douay-Rheims)

Blessed *be* the God and Father of our Lord Jesus Christ, who has blessed us with every spiritual blessing in the heavenly *places*.... (NKJV)

Blessed be the God and Father of our Lord Jesus Christ, who has blessed us with every spiritual blessing in the heavens.... (HCSB)

All praise to God, the Father of our Lord Jesus Christ, who has blessed us with every spiritual blessing in the heavenly realms.... (NLT)

Praise the God and Father of our Lord Jesus Christ for the spiritual blessings that Christ has brought us from heaven! (CEV)

How blessed is God! And what a blessing he is! He's the Father of our Master, Jesus Christ, and takes us to the high places of blessing in him. (The Message)

OUTSIDE INFLUENCES ON TRANSLATION CHOICES

Various extraneous considerations can influence translations of the Bible. One, as noted in the example at the beginning of chapter 5, is the matter of propriety in language. What would be a coarse expression in English — "any that pisseth against the wall" — and would therefore not be read aloud in churches, is mitigated by a paraphrase in most modern translations, even those that are otherwise closest to a word-for-word rendering, such as the New American Standard Bible.

Theological influence over translation choices can also arise. The most famous of such passages is Isaiah 7.14, translated either "a young woman shall conceive," or "a virgin shall conceive" in accordance with the quotation of this verse in

Matthew 1.23. As many people have pointed out, the original Hebrew text of Isaiah uses a word — 'almah — that means "a woman old enough to marry," and there is a different Hebrew word *(bethulah)* that means "virgin." The ancient Greek translation of the Hebrew Bible, the Septuagint, used the Greek word *parthenos* ("virgin") in translating this passage, and that word was picked up in early Christian writings and treated as a prediction of Jesus' birth from a virgin mother. It may be that *parthenos* did not necessarily carry the technical sense meaning "never having had sexual intercourse." It could be a word, like the English "maiden," that had such a meaning but was sometimes used inexactly. (Other Greek translations of the Hebrew Bible, probably in response to this Christian use of the text, translated the Hebrew word by the Greek word *neanis,* "young woman," in order to undercut the argument.)

The word "virgin," however, did make it into Matthew's gospel in a quotation of this verse, and most evangelical Protestant translations have used that fact to justify the choice of "virgin" as a translation in the original verse in Isaiah:

> Again the LORD spoke to Ahaz, "Ask the LORD your God for a sign, whether in the deepest depths or in the highest heights."
>
> But Ahaz said, "I will not ask; I will not put the LORD to the test."
>
> Then Isaiah said, "Hear now, you house of David! Is it not enough to try the patience of men? Will you try the patience of my God also? Therefore the Lord himself will give you a sign: The virgin will be with child and will give birth to a son, and will call him Immanuel.... But before the boy knows enough to reject the wrong and choose the right, the land of the two kings you dread will be laid waste." (7.10–14, 16, NIV)

In doing so, they are implicitly making the point that the original context and usage in Isaiah (in which the birth is meant as a sign to King Ahaz of something that will happen within two years or so) must be subordinated to the later Christian use of this verse as a prediction of Jesus' birth, which in Isaiah's time would not have made sense as a sign for what was going to happen in the not-so-distant future.

The specific history of an audience, and the need to be sensitive to it, can also influence translation choices. A good example of cultural sensitivity in translation occurs in the various word choices for "servant" or "slave" when translating the New Testament. In Greek, the word *doulos* generally means "slave" — that is, "bondservant" — and there is a different word, *diakonos,* that means "servant," with no implication that the person is the property of a master. In addition, in Greek as in other languages (compare French *garçon*), the word "child" or "boy" — *pais* — can also be used for "servant." Other words exist for slaves captured in war, for house-servants, and so on.

If we were to translate according to formal, word-for-word criteria, we would always translate *doulos* as "slave" and *diakonos* as "servant." There are passages where *doulos* refers to a specific circumstance, or in which a particular person is meant, and in those cases it is often translated "slave." For example, in Matthew 8.9, in the incident of the healing of the centurion's servant (here *pais*), the centurion says to Jesus, in reference to his own authority, "I say... to my slave *[doulō mou]* 'Do this....'" In this instance, the person being spoken of is someone in a specific historical circumstance. The New American Standard Bible, the New American Bible, and the New Revised Standard Version all render the word here as "slave." (Other translations, such as the New International Version, following the practice of the King James Version, generally render *doulos* as "servant" no matter where it appears.)

In Galatians 1.10, however, in a passage where Paul is speaking of his own relationship to Christ, the word occurs again — but this time in a usage that is metaphorical, and one which also is meant to be applicable to the audience, and therefore to Christians generally. Paul refers to himself as the *doulos* of Christ. Here, while the New American Bible uses "slave" and the New American Standard Bible says "bond-servant," the New Revised Standard Version renders it as "servant." Why? Because the translation is trying to accommodate the fact that such passages will be read aloud in churches, including congregations that include African Americans or that are part of historically black denominations. To use the word "slave" here, and ask people to apply it to themselves, even in relation to Christ, is to risk being insensitive to the history of African Americans in this country.

Finally, the use of a biblical text in a liturgical or prayer context can sometimes work backwards to influence the way the text itself is translated, because people wish to read familiar phrases in their Bibles. One instance of this has occurred in some translations of Luke 1.28, the beginning of the angel Gabriel's Annunciation to Mary:

> Hail, *kecharitomene!* The Lord is with you!

The Greek word means "one who has been given *charis* [grace, favor]." It is possible to look at this in two ways: the person as the object of grace-giving, or the person as graced. Many translations take the first approach and translate "favored one" (such as the New American Bible sponsored by the U. S. Catholic Church) or "you who enjoy God's favour" (the New Jerusalem Bible, used in many Catholic churches in Great Britain and Commonwealth countries). The traditional Rheims New Testament, however, followed Jerome's Vulgate, which translated this word as *gratia plena,* "full of grace," the phrasing that is followed in the traditional prayer, *Ave Maria.* That approach is followed in some modern Catholic translations. When the Revised Standard Version was being adapted for use by Catholics (a task mostly of rearranging the Old Testament), the Catholic scholars who undertook the task also made adjustments in the New Testament. The standard Revised Standard Version read "Hail, O favored one," but the Catholic Revised Standard Version now reads, "Hail, full of grace."

THE LIMITS OF FORMAL, WORD-FOR-WORD TRANSLATION: MARK 5:21-43

Two renderings of a Markan narrative (5.21–43) show the limits of a literal approach and also demonstrate what a very free translation can attempt to accomplish. The literal rendering, which I have supplied in order to make matters as clear as possible, reproduces three of Mark's characteristic features of style:

his simple linkages of events using sentences beginning with "and"; his sense of immediacy, indicated by repetition of "right away"; and his use of the "historical present" (the present tense in a context that clearly makes it past tense, which in English is highly informal, usually spoken, style). The combination of these elements, when rendered literally, makes Mark seem overly naïve, even childish, in English. I have reproduced a fairly lengthy passage, including one story being interrupted by another, in order to show how a literal rendering of Mark's style would really sound if carried out consistently.

> And Jesus crossing over again [by boat] to the other side a big crowd gathered by him, and he was by the sea. And one of the synagogue rulers comes to him, named Jairus, and seeing him he falls at his feet and begs him a lot saying, "My little daughter is near the end, so that you lay your hands on her so that she can get well and live." So he went with him. And a big crowd was going with him and pressing on him. And a woman having blood flow twelve years — and she suffered under many doctors and spent all she had and didn't get better but worse — and hearing about Jesus, came up behind in the crowd and touched his cloak; because she said, "If I just touch his clothes I'll be whole." And right away her blood flow dried up and she knew in her body that she was healed from that disease. And right away Jesus knowing in himself that power had gone out of him turned around in the crowd and said, "Who touched my clothes?" And his disciples said to him, "You see the crowd pressing on you and you say, 'Who touched me'?" And he looked around to see the one who had done this. But the woman fearing and trembling, knowing what had happened in her, came and fell down before him and told him the whole truth. But he said to her, "Daughter, your faith has made you whole; go in peace and be healed of that disease." While he was still speaking they come from the synagogue ruler's saying, "Your daughter has died; why bother the teacher anymore?" But Jesus overhearing the word they were saying says to the synagogue ruler, "Don't be afraid, only believe." And he allowed no one to follow him but Peter and James and John the brother of James. And they come to the house of the synagogue ruler and he sees a

to-do and a lot of weeping and wailing, and coming in he says to them, "Why make a to-do and weep? The child has not died but sleeps." And they laughing at him, but he throwing out all of them, he takes with him the father of the child and the mother and those with him and goes into where the child was. And taking the hand of the child he says to her, "Talitha kum," which is translated, "Little girl, I say to you, get up." And right away the little girl rose and walked around, since she was twelve years old. And they were astounded with great astonishment. And he strictly ordered them so that nobody should know all this, and he said to give her something to eat. *(fairly literal rendering)*

The same passage as translated in The Message retains the sense of immediacy without conveying immaturity. One aspect of this translation is of particular interest. The Message is an effort not merely to translate words, but to convey a sense of what the passage might have meant to its original audience. In the next-to-last paragraph, therefore, the translator has rendered not just the words but the cultural references as well. In the land of Jesus' time, standing outside the house where someone has died and weeping audibly were ways of expressing sympathy. That is not the case in present-day America; people are more likely to bring prepared food to a house where someone has died (and, of course, some people just come around to be able to say they had been there and to relate any juicy items they might hear). The translator, therefore, has substituted for the weepers "gossips looking for a story and neighbors bringing in casseroles." "Gossips" and "casseroles" are not in the Greek text, but they are intended to produce an effect on a contemporary audience similar to the one that Mark's original audience might have felt.

After Jesus crossed over by boat, a large crowd met him at the seaside. One of the meeting-place leaders named Jairus came. When he saw Jesus, he fell to his knees, beside himself as he begged, "My dear daughter is at death's door. Come and lay hands on her so she will get well and live." Jesus went with him, the whole crowd tagging along, pushing and jostling him.

A woman who had suffered a condition of hemorrhaging for twelve years — a long succession of physicians had treated her, and treated her badly, taking all her money and leaving her worse off than before — had heard about Jesus. She slipped in from behind and touched his robe. She was thinking to herself, "If I can put a finger on his robe, I can get well." The moment she did it, the flow of blood dried up. She could feel the change, and knew her plague was over and done with.

At the same moment, Jesus felt energy discharging from him. He turned around to the crowd and asked, "Who touched my robe?"

His disciples said, "What are you talking about? With this crowd pushing and jostling you, you're asking, 'Who touched me?' Dozens have touched you!"

But he went on asking, looking around to see who had done it. The woman, knowing what had happened, knowing she was the one, stepped up in fear and trembling, knelt before him, and gave him the whole story.

Jesus said to her, "Daughter, you took a risk of faith, and now you're healed and whole. Live well, live blessed! Be healed of your plague."

While he was still talking, some people came from the leader's house and told him, "Your daughter is dead. Why bother the Teacher any more?"

Jesus overheard what they were talking about and said to the leader, "Don't listen to them; just trust me."

He permitted no one to go in with him except Peter, James, and John. They entered the leader's house and pushed their way through the gossips looking for a story and neighbors bringing in casseroles. Jesus was abrupt: "Why all this busy-body grief and gossip? This child isn't dead; she's sleeping." Provoked to sarcasm, they told him he didn't know what he was talking about.

But when he had sent them all out, he took the child's father and mother, along with his companions, and entered the child's room. He clasped the girl's hand and said, *"Talitha koum,"* which means, "Little girl, get up." At that, she was up and walking around! This girl was twelve years of age. They, of course, were all beside themselves with joy. He gave them strict orders that no one was to know what had taken place in that room. Then he said, "Give her something to eat." (The Message)

THE IMPORTANCE OF ATTENDING TO CULTURE-SPECIFIC REFERENCES

While "casseroles" might seem like a stretch, it is actually very important for translators to take into account culture-specific references that can mislead the reader. For example, a number of passages in the Hebrew Bible use the word *kelayoth* — "kidneys" — or its first-person singular possessive form *kilyotay*, "my kidneys." Translators must decide in each case how literally they are going to translate this word. In Psalm 16.7, for example, the King James Version translates, "my reins also instruct me in the night seasons." Perhaps only one in a hundred people today, unless instructed in archaic meanings in English, would be able to explain the meaning of this phrase. Rendered into modern English, it would be, "My kidneys teach me during the night." ("Reins" in the English of King James's time was derived from the Latin word *renes*, which means "kidneys" and is the root of the modern English medical term "renal.") If we were to translate the verse using "kidneys," it would be meaningless, or worse, misleading to a modern reader, maybe bringing to mind thoughts of midnight trips to the bathroom.

That is not, however, what the verse means. The Hebrew word does mean "kidneys," the internal organs, and in passages such as Leviticus 3.4 ("the two kidneys with the fat that is on them") the literal meaning is the correct one. But in Hebrew "kidneys" also meant "the innermost being," the place where one's life is centered. That is the meaning in Psalm 16, and most modern translations render it as "my heart teaches me... ."

So much for Psalm 16. If we have decided that in metaphorical passages "kidneys" in Hebrew means "heart" in English, we are then confronted with Psalm 26.2. The second half of this verse reads, in a literal translation, "test my kidneys and heart." Obviously "heart and heart" will not do as a translation, and so most modern versions render it "heart and mind" — thus giving metaphorical and less physical sense to words that are quite

obviously, at root, physical in Hebrew — and, incidentally, drop-
ping the literal rendering of "heart" in favor of a metaphorical
translation for that word as well.

Finally, there is a passage such as the following from Job:

> God gives me up to the ungodly,
>   and casts me into the hands of the wicked.
> I was at ease, and he broke me in two;
>   he seized me by the neck and dashed me to pieces;
> he set me up as his target;
>   his archers surround me.
> He slashes open my kidneys, and shows no mercy;
>   he pours out my gall on the ground.
> He bursts upon me again and again;
>   he rushes at me like a warrior. (16.11–14, NRSV)

Clearly all of these images of torment are meant metaphorical-
ly. Even in the context of Job's extravagant language, and the
book's presentation of his very real suffering — emotional, psychological, spiritual, and physical — his body is not broken, nor
is it broken open. The meaning of the phrase "he slashes open
my kidneys" is "he cuts into my very life" or words to that effect.
The Revised English Bible, for instance, translates this line, "he
pierced deep into my vitals." That perhaps conveys the
metaphorical sense while keeping the idea of pain at least equal
to the most excruciating physical injury.

To get a sense of the overlap here between the physical and
the spiritual or psychological, we can reflect on English usage
of the word "stomach" in various contexts. In the phrase "stomach trouble" the reference is usually a physical one; by comparison, if someone says, "I don't have the stomach for that job," the
meaning is metaphorical, but the sense of distaste or nausea is
clearly in the background. Likewise with "heart attack" — purely physical — and "Have a heart!" — metaphorical. A sense
somewhere between these two might be represented in the
phrase "My heart stood still." In this last usage, "heart" is
metaphorical: the speaker's heart did not literally stop. But the
physical sense is hovering close by, since a sudden shock, even
good news when unexpected and delivered out of the blue, can

cause a physical sensation that *feels* like one's heart has stopped.

The same is the case with the passage from Job. The meaning is clearly metaphorical: Job's kidneys are, in fact, intact and uninjured. But the meaning is that his suffering is, on the spiritual or emotional level, the equivalent of a mortal wound to his innermost vital organs. Conveying this kind of double meaning is one of the hardest tasks of translation.

CHANGE IS GOOD

Consideration of all of these examples should make it clear that translation, especially of a text as complex as the Bible, needs to take multiple needs into account in deciding how words, phrases, and even passages and entire books must be rendered into English. It should also be clear that choosing one translation approach does not just preclude other approaches; it also precludes other experiences of the text. If we translate the text in a literal, word-for-word fashion, the reader's experience of the translation is not going to be the same sort of experience as that of the original audience. The present-day reader will see the text as exotic, as removed in time and culture, and perhaps for those reasons as beautiful, antique, and romantic. If we translate according to a meaning-for-meaning approach, we will be able to present the text as speaking directly to readers of the present as it spoke directly to readers or hearers in the past; but we will lose, or at least minimize, the fact that the text itself is ancient and foreign.

It is for this reason above all that professionals, at least, should regularly use more than one translation. Even those who can read the ancient languages, unless they are very adept, should open themselves to the experience of reading the efforts of others in rendering the Bible into modern English. And even more, in preaching and teaching they should present to their hearers a broad array of renderings from time to time. There is an advantage in using one translation consistently for the lectionary readings: For those members of the congregation who gather week after week, year after year, the repetitions eventually become familiar and the texts sink into the mind and become part of their thoughts almost beneath their awareness. But it is not always a good thing to leave something out of awareness. Sometimes a change, even a shocking change, can be healthy. Offering a different translation in the sermon, trying out a different translation for a season of the year, and — particularly — using a variety of translations in teaching, can all bring new light to bear on texts that might otherwise have become overly familiar. A congregation that has been used to hearing "Blessed *are* the poor in spirit, for theirs is the kingdom of heaven" (Matt. 5.3, KJV) and nodding contentedly at the old words might suddenly sit up in surprise if, instead, they heard "God blesses those who are poor and realize their need for him, for the Kingdom of Heaven is theirs" (NLT), or "You're blessed when you're at the end of your rope. With less of you there is more of God and his rule" (The Message). A translation cannot, by itself, make anyone think; but a change in translation might at least get people talking about what a passage means. And conveying meaning is the ultimate task of translation.

Chapter 7

❧ CHOOSING
A TRANSLATION

NOW THAT WE have looked at many of the issues that arise in Bible translations, we can turn to the question of choosing a good translation for a specific purpose. This is a matter of making sure that the translation fits the use you have in mind for it, and that it is appropriate for the audience or readers who will be using it.

The easiest issue to deal with is finding a translation that is acceptable to the group that will be using it. (See "Differing Canons," pp. 10ff.) Roman Catholics need a translation that has been approved by some official body for use by Catholics. Many evangelical Christians do not want to use a Bible that includes the Apocrypha, since they do not regard those books as legitimate parts of the Bible. Jews will use only a translation of the Hebrew Bible. The descriptions in the chart of various translations generally available (p. 9) and in the brief guide to translations at the end of this book (pp. 89ff.) include the primary audience for which the translation was undertaken. In most cases, however, narrowing the range to a particular religious type of the translation will still leave you with a broad range of choices, and more specific criteria are needed when selecting a translation to use.

TRANSLATIONS TO BE HEARD

First, ask yourself how the translation will be used. Will people primarily be hearing it, or reading it? If they will be hearing it, the sentence structure cannot be too complex, or it will be difficult to grasp the meaning. In the case of lectionary readings or other, similar uses in church services, the translation also needs to fit the style of the surrounding worship text.

For informal services — youth group prayers, for example — a translation like The Message, with its idiomatic style and contemporary "feel," might be a good choice. For somewhat more formal occasions — a Bible reading at a congregational meeting, an ecumenical prayer service — the New Living Translation, the Contemporary English Version, or some similar rendering would work well. For regular lectionary readings with a set worship book — the *Book of Common Prayer,* the *Lutheran Book of Worship,* and other standard liturgies — the Revised Standard Version, New Revised Standard Version, or (for non-Anglicans, since Anglicans need to have the Apocrypha for lectionary purposes) the New International Version would serve well. Lutherans also generally prefer to have a Bible version that includes the Apocrypha, since Luther translated those additional books.

Finally, for very traditional occasions, such as Christmas pageants, funerals where many elderly people will be present, traditional weddings, or prayer services at the occasion of some national tragedy, the King James Version might be the best choice. Particularly for familiar passages — the nativity story from Luke, the opening of the Gospel of John, Psalm 23, the Hymn to Love in 1 Corinthians 13, Ruth's vow from the book of Ruth — the King James Version still has a cultural resonance and an appeal to memory that reaches people who otherwise know little of the Bible. On occasions when those who seldom or never attend church will be a significant part of the congregation, that quality can be critically important. For groups where the assembly will be younger and will include evangelical Protestants, the New King James Version can also be a good choice.

TRANSLATIONS TO BE READ

If the translation is primarily for reading by oneself or in the context of a group discussion or study session, then you might consider more formal translations. The Revised Standard Version (for mainline Protestants and Catholics), the New American Bible (for Catholics), and the New American Standard Bible (for evangelical Protestants) are all good choices for classes where word-study, verbal echoes within the text, and other aspects brought out in word-for-word translations are an advantage. For contrast, versions such as those of Moffatt and Phillips provide provocative renderings of the original texts that can help stimulate thought and discussion.

ASSESSING A NEW TRANSLATION

How can you tell what sort of translation any particular Bible version is? There are several places to look for clues before you engage in any direct comparison with another version. The description given on the back cover or jacket will probably indicate which kind of reading the translation is designed for. If the description stresses accuracy and authenticity, the translation is likely to be on the word-for-word end of the spectrum. If it emphasizes readability, it is probably a meaning-for-meaning rendition. Translations that fall in the middle range generally try to touch both ends: they will have descriptions such as "clear and accurate," "faithful to the original texts yet expressed in beautiful English," and other phrases appealing both to those looking for a word-for-word translation and to those who want a meaning-for-meaning version.

The preface or introduction will also afford clues. Most translations nowadays do not directly attack other versions, but implicitly they will criticize approaches that differ from the one they chose. For example, the Preface to the New King James Version says, "Dynamic equivalence, a recent procedure in Bible translation, commonly results in paraphrasing. . . ." Prefaces may also offer examples of translation choices that will serve to indicate which category of translation they belong to.

Finally, nothing is better than sitting down with a version and comparing significant passages to other versions. You should try both familiar and unfamiliar passages, and seek out difficult as well as simpler ones. The Psalms and Job will indicate how well the translation can handle poetry, and historical accounts — particularly Samuel or Acts — will show how it handles prose narrative. Passages from the New Testament letters will indicate how well argument and complex sentences can be conveyed in English; it is usually in these texts that formal translations demonstrate their adherence to principle most clearly. Gospel stories are often fairly simple in their sentence structure, and there may not be much difference between the ways in which different versions render them; but the letters, with their complex syntax, are another matter. You can also check the translators' footnotes: if they offer many "literal" renderings, then the translation itself is likely to be a more formal, word-for-word one.

CONCLUSION

It may be helpful, in a final overview of the issues we have explored here, to present translation choices in terms of another metaphor. We began by comparing translations to knives, as a way of grasping that individual translations are designed for specific uses, and it is important to understand the use to which a translation is to be put before judging its success or failure as a translation. There are as many different kinds of translations as there are different kinds of knives — because there are different tasks to be accomplished.

There are many other ways of looking at translation. Perhaps it will be clearer if we look at the various versions resulting from different translation approaches as buildings. One approach, that of a formal and literal rendering, represents the Bible as purely as possible as an ancient writing arising in a culture very different from our own: in other words, as a museum. Ancient Hebrew practices and even verbal characteristics, Greco-Roman patriarchal arrangements, Greek syntax — all are faithfully reproduced on the page, just as ancient artifacts can be displayed in a museum case. The result is like a visit to a collection of exotic and rare objects: informative, interesting, enlightening, but also remote from ordinary experience and daily living.

The other approach, the dynamic and functional one, looks at the ancient texts and tries to recreate in today's terms the experience of how they might originally have been read: the translators are seeking to build a home in which contemporary readers feel comfortable. With this approach, idiosyncrasies of ancient culture are minimized and the translator makes an effort to understand how an original reader or hearer of the text might have reacted to it, and how someone living today can experience the text in a similar way. In effect, the translators are trying to see how we can "feel at home" in a passage from Job or Romans. Reading one of these translations provides a sense of immediacy, of a contemporaneous text, while the Bible's character as a collection of ancient writings recedes into the background.

The choice in translations, then, is between visiting a museum and building a home. Each is of value and each provides something the other cannot. A museum, by giving its visitors opportunities beyond what they will meet in their everyday lives, provides them with the tools to enlarge their experiences and thereby to grow. It is broadening and educational. A home is meant to provide comfort and shelter. It is familiar, and provides the background for one's ordinary life. To be sure, a home can contain exotic objects: souvenirs from travel, even rare and foreign ornaments. And a museum can be comfortable and even familiar, placing everyday items or contemporary objects in displays that show off their characteristics in new ways. But each serves a purpose of its own, and each is needed for a full life.

Someone who never leaves home, who cannot abide the strange and challenging, is living a truncated existence. Someone who must always live among rare and exotic objects, who cannot function in the mundane, becomes increasingly remote from the lives most of us lead. We need the security of the everyday, and we need the experience of those whose "everyday" was different from ours. We can learn from people and places very far from those we regularly inhabit, and we can return to our own locales with renewed vision and better understanding of their true character.

So it should be with our use of Bible translations. We need ones that clarify for us the Bible's ancient character, and the differences between its culture and ours. And even when the text is familiar, we need to be reminded that it grew out of a situation very different from our own, so that we can grasp the critical point that our human nature and God's interactions with us are not culturally bound, however much they must express themselves in the terms of a particular culture. At the same time, we need translations that make the connection between our lives and the Bible's settings as clear as possible. This does not mean that a given translation cannot have anything foreign or exotic — an ancient meal will still be cooked over an open fire, though the hunger it will assuage is the same as our own.

We need both kinds of experiences in our reading of the Bible: translations that are deeply rooted in the everyday and those that reach out into the full human family; translations that can seem to arise out of our local lives and ones that draw upon the whole inhabited world, past and present.

❧ FURTHER READING

An excellent guide to issues involved with inclusive language translation is:
Carson, D.A. *The Inclusive Language Debate.* Grand Rapids: Baker Book House, 1998. 221 pp.

Sometimes the best way to compare different translations is by using a parallel Bible or parallel New Testament text. The following are currently available:

Hendrickson Parallel Bible. Peabody, MA: Hendrickson Publishers, Inc., 2005. 2880 pp.
King James Version, New King James Version, New International Version, New Living Translation.

Laymen's Parallel Bible. Grand Rapids: Zondervan Publishing, Inc., 1991. 3136 pp.
King James Version, New International Version, The Living Bible, New Revised Standard Version.

People's Parallel Bible. Wheaton, IL: Tyndale Publishers, 1982. 1600 pp.
King James Version, The Living Bible.

Today's Parallel Bible. Grand Rapids, MI: Zondervan, 2000. 2880 pp.
New International Version, King James Version, New American Standard Bible, New Living Translation.

The following parallel editions include explanatory materials as well as the translations themselves.

Kohlenberger, John R., III, ed. *Essential Evangelical Parallel Bible.* New York: Oxford University Press, 2004. 2945 pp.
New King James Version, English Standard Version, New Living Translation, The Message.

―――. *Catholic Comparative New Testament.* New York: Oxford University Press, 2005. 1762 pp.
Douay-Rheims, Revised Standard Version Catholic edition, New American Bible, New Revised Standard Version Catholic edition (Anglicized), Jerusalem Bible, Good News Translation, New Jerusalem Bible, Christian Community Bible.

―――. *Contemporary Parallel New Testament.* New York: Oxford University Press, 1997. 1787 pp.
King James Version, New American Standard Bible, New Century Version, Contemporary English Version, New International Version, New Living Translation, New King James Version, The Message.

―――. *Evangelical Parallel New Testament.* New York: Oxford University Press, 2003. 1727 pp.
New King James Version, New International Version, English Standard Version, Holman Christian Standard Bible, Today's New International Version, New Living Translation, New Century Version, The Message.

―――. *The Parallel Apocrypha.* New York: Oxford University Press, 1997. 1188 pp.
Greek (Septuagint), King James Version, Douay, Knox, Today's English Version, New Revised Standard Version, New American Bible, New Jerusalem Bible. Includes six essays on the Apocrypha in Judaism, Orthodox Christianity, Catholicism, Anglicanism, mainline Protestantism, and evangelical Protestantism.

A QUICK GUIDE TO BIBLE TRANSLATIONS AND ABBREVIATIONS

Dates given are generally those of the publication of the full Bible or of the latest edition.

Alter — ***The Five Books of Moses* by Robert Alter** (2004): a translation by a noted literary critic and student of the Hebrew Bible, whose writings on Hebrew prose and poetical style have had wide influence. Alter's translation is highly formal, but also poetical and sensitive to both Hebrew and English usage. Example: "Let me sing unto the LORD for He surged, O surged — / horse and its rider He hurled into the sea. / My strength and my power is Yah, / and He became my deliverance" (Exodus 15.1-2).

ASV — **American Standard Version** (1901): a translation produced by American scholars who had worked on the British **Revised Version.** This translation then became the basis of the **Revised Standard Version** and the **New American Standard Bible.**

CEV — **Contemporary English Version** (1995): a project of the American Bible Society. A revision of **Today's English Version.**

Douay Bible   **Douay-Rheims Bible** (New Testament, 1582; complete Bible, 1609–10; revised edition by Bishop Challoner, 1749–52): the traditional Roman Catholic English translation. The Douay Bible, as it is often called, is a translation from the Vulgate with reference to the original Greek and Hebrew, undertaken by English scholars who did not convert to Anglicanism during the sixteenth century English reformation. The Douay Bible tends to use Latin-influenced vocabulary: "Give us this day our supersubstantial bread" (Matthew 6.11).

ESV   **English Standard Version** (2001): an adaptation of the **Revised Standard Version** by a group of evangelical Protestant scholars, which updates some archaic language in the Revised Standard Version and makes some adjustments to reflect evangelical theological understandings.

Fox   ***The Five Books of Moses* by Everett Fox** (1995): A rendering of the Hebrew Bible by the Jewish scholar Everett Fox that aims to reflect in English the structure and "feel" of the Bible in Hebrew. Examples: "The human said: This-time, she-is-it! Bone from my bones, flesh from my flesh! She shall be called Woman/*Isha,* for from Man/*Ish* she was taken!" (Genesis 2:23). "The snake said to the woman: Die, you will not die!" (Genesis 3.4).

Good News   **Good News for Modern Man:** another title for **Today's English Version,** also known simply as the Good News Bible.

HCSB   **Holman Christian Standard Bible** (2004): a project of the Southern Baptist Convention, working through the Southern Baptist Sunday School Board and its publisher, Holman. The HCSB aims to be a precise rendering of the original languages for use in churches and Bible study groups.

JB and NJB   **The Jerusalem Bible** (1965) and **The New Jerusalem Bible** (1985): these British Catholic translations are based on the original Greek and Hebrew texts, but they draw inspiration from a modern French

Catholic translation, *La Bible de Jerusalem*. The Jerusalem Bible and New Jerusalem Bible translations are among the most poetical English versions. J. R. R. Tolkien was among the literary scholars who advised the Jerusalem Bible translators on style.

KJV

King James Version (1611; revised 1769 and 1884): the traditional English Protestant Bible, sometimes called the Authorized Version because it was authorized for reading in the Church of England in the seventeenth century. The King James Version is largely a formal translation, but it also employs paraphrase. It includes the Apocrypha, although most published versions omit it.

Knox

The Holy Bible **by Ronald Knox (1950):** Msgr. Ronald Knox was a well-known literary writer and a famous Catholic convert in the first half of the twentieth century; his father was an Anglican bishop, and one of his brothers was an Anglican priest. The Knox translation is based on the Vulgate, the Latin translation of St. Jerome. It is beautifully literary, almost rhythmical in many passages.

The Message

The Message (2003): a project of the Rev. Eugene Peterson, a Protestant minister. The Message is the translation that is closest to a paraphrase. It is well-suited for those new to the Bible, but it should be used cautiously for scholarly work because it frequently goes beyond what is actually in the text.

Moffatt

The Bible **by James Moffatt** (1934): Professor James Moffatt was a prominent English biblical scholar during the first half of the twentieth century. This translation utilizes modern scholarship, and often rearranges the order of the text to demonstrate the various units of which it is composed, or to show how the text can be reconstructed. It is often poetical. Example: "Where is wisdom to be found? And knowledge, where does it abound?" (Job 28.1). Prof. Moffatt was one of the translators of the **Revised Standard Version,** and for that translation he advocated a more formal approach.

NAB

New American Bible (1991): the official translation of the United States Conference of Catholic Bishops (USCCB), translated largely by Catholic scholars who are members of the Catholic Biblical Association. The New American Bible is a generally formal translation, but is quite readable. It is accompanied in most editions by introductions and extensive notes to the text, in keeping with the Catholic Church's teaching that the Bible should be presented to the reader in the context of church teaching and scholarship. The Old Testament is currently being revised.

NASB

New American Standard Bible (1995): a revision by evangelical Protestant scholars of the **American Standard Version** of 1901. The NASB is the most consistently formal translation generally available. It is sometimes difficult reading, but that reflects the underlying texts.

NCV

New Century Version (1991): a project of the World Bible Translation Center and other evangelical Protestant scholars. The New Century Version uses a limited vocabulary, wherever possible, to make its renderings accessible to younger readers and to those for whom English is not their first language. It also offers explanatory footnotes for difficult terms (when these cannot be avoided) and ancient customs, and renders measurements into modern equivalents. It is consequently very readable.

NEB and REB

New English Bible (1970) and Revised English Bible (1989): a project of the British Council of Churches, the New English Bible was the first major English translation since the sixteenth century to begin afresh, without reference to previous translations. It is poetical and literary in a high degree, and, while not always easy, is generally readable. It was revised and published as the Revised English Bible in 1989.

NET Bible

New English Translation (2001): a project of a group of evangelical Protestant scholars, the NET Bible provides the reader with extensive notes that explain the nuances of the underlying original language terms.

NIV

New International Version (1978; revised 1984): a project of the International Bible Society and a group of Protestant evangelical scholars. The New International Version is a middle-of-the-road translation, an evangelical counterpart to the **Revised Standard Version.** After the **King James Version,** it is the most popular Protestant version.

NJPS

New Jewish Publication Society translation, "Tanakh" (1985): a project of the Jewish Publication Society, the "Tanakh" or New Jewish Publication Society translation is the standard scholarly rendition of the Hebrew Scriptures for Jewish readers. It follows the Jewish order for the books of the Bible; the content is the same as the Protestant Old Testament. The New Jewish Publication Society translation is generally formal, but dynamic in places and very readable.

NKJV

New King James Version (1982): an updated rendering of the **King James Version,** which eliminates archaisms while trying to preserve essential elements of the King James Version. The New King James Version is the only modern translation that does not use a current Greek text, but follows the King James Version in using the *textus receptus,* the Greek text established during the early Renaissance.

NLT

New Living Translation (1996; revised 2004): a new version of a classic paraphrase, The Living Bible. Dr. Kenneth Taylor paraphrased the Bible for use with his own children; this edition is the result of the efforts of Protestant evangelical scholars to update and revise that book, keeping its readability while making it more accurate.

NRSV

New Revised Standard Version (1989): a full revision of the **Revised Standard Version.** It is still, along with the Revised Standard Version, the only translation that includes every book regarded as part of the Bible by one or more of the various Christian churches.

Phillips
The New Testament in Modern English by J. B. **Phillips** (1958): J. B. Phillips was an Anglican clergyman who worked among the poor in English cities; this translation grew out of his work with inner-city youth. It is readable and energetic; like **The Message,** it occasionally goes beyond what is in the text to make the meaning clearer to contemporary readers.

RSV
Revised Standard Version (New Testament, 1946; Old and New Testaments, 1952; Apocrypha, 1957; New Testament second edition, 1971; expanded Apocrypha, 1977): the first major post-World War II English translation, which largely replaced the **King James Version** in mainline Protestant churches in the 1950s. It was sponsored by the National Council of Churches, and appeared in editions for Catholics and Orthodox Christians. Its translation committee was fully ecumenical, including Protestant, Catholic, and Orthodox scholars, and interfaith, with a Jewish scholar as well.

RV
Revised Version (New Testament, 1881; full Bible including Apocrypha, 1885): a British translation intended to update the **King James Version** both in the textual basis for the New Testament and in its language. It is probably the most formal translation ever to receive wide dissemination, but it failed ultimately to supplant the King James Version. The American variant of this translation published in 1901 is the **American Standard Version.**

TEV
Today's English Version (latest edition, 1992): a project of the American Bible Society. Today's English Version was intended as a simplified-language translation for those new to the Bible, and particularly for those whose first language is not English. It is readable, with simplified sentence structure. It has also been published under the title *Good News for Modern Man* and is also known as the Good News Bible.

TNIV
Today's New International Version (2001): a revision of the NIV, partly to adjust the language to make it more gender-inclusive with regard to human beings.

Copyright notes

Quotations from the various translations are, with the exception of those from the King James Version, the Douay-Rheims Bible, and the Revised Version, copyright by the following publishers. In all cases, the copyright owners reserve all rights.

The Bible: A New Translation by James A. R. Moffatt. © 1922, 1924, 1925, 1926, 1935 by Harper & Row, Publishers, Inc.; copyright © 1950, 1952, 1953, 1954 by James A. R. Moffatt.

The Contemporary English Version © 1995 by The American Bible Society.

English Standard Version © 2001 by Crossway Bibles, a division of Good News Publishers. Used by permission.

The Five Books of Moses by Everett Fox © 1983, 1986, 1990, 1995 by Schocken Books, Inc.

Holman Christian Standard Bible © 1999, 2000, 2002, 2004 by Holman Bible Publishers. Used by permission.

The Holy Bible translated by Ronald Knox © 1944, 1948, 1950 by Sheed & Ward, Inc., New York.

The Message: The Bible in Contemporary Language © 2003 by Eugene H. Peterson. Used by permission of NavPress Publishing Group.

New American Bible © 1970 by the Confraternity of Christian Doctrine (CCD), Washington, D. C. (1 Samuel through 2 Maccabees copyright © 1969); *Revised New Testament of the New American Bible* © 1986 by the CCD; *Revised Psalms of the New American Bible* © 1991 by the CCD.

New American Standard Bible © 1960, 1962, 1963, 1968, 1971, 1972, 1973, 1975, 1977, 1995 by The Lockman Foundation. Used by permission.

New Century Version © 1987, 1988, 1991 by Word Publishing, a division of Thomas Nelson, Inc. Used by permission.

The New English Bible © 1961, 1970 by the Delegates of the Oxford University Press and the Syndics of the Cambridge University Press.

New International Version © 1973, 1978, 1984 by International Bible Society. Used by permission of Zondervan.

BASEMENT